THE COURAGE

Learning How to Develop

to LEAD

Compassion
Character
Critical Thinking
Common Sense
Courage

Derrick Boles

THE COURAGE

to

LEAD

Derrick Boles

The Courage to Lead

By Derrick Boles

Editor: Amy Larson

Formatting & Interior Design: Renee Settle & Aspen Morrow

Project Management, PR & Production: Pottenger Press & Publicity

ISBN: 9780986443206

ISBN: 9780986443213 CS Amazon POD

ASIN Kindle: B00Q7H5JVO

Second Printing

4JPublishing

DEDICATION

Dedicated to my late mother
Norma Nell Boles (Woods)

"DON'T FIND FAULT, FIND
A REMEDY"
--HENRY FORD

CONTENTS

MEET

DERRICK BOLES

Derrick Boles was raised by his mother and in the absence of a father, typical for many children in Detroit at the time. Due to socio-economic and family structure, he felt pegged as one whose future had already been mapped out, with the likelihood of either incarceration or early death to the violence of the streets.

The shallow view of others was one of the things that propelled Derrick out of the pessimistic box he'd been placed in, as he ignored the bleak prospect that children like him would never become truly great individuals.

As talent for athletics evidenced, mentors played a large role in Boles' emergence, assisting him with intense training, and offering deep lessons on life and becoming a responsible adult. Wanting to excel in sports, Derrick Boles promised God one night while alone on a running track that he'd do whatever was asked, if only he was granted the chance to become a professional basketball player. A few months later, Derrick signed his first contract to play international basketball in Taiwan.

He went on to become a diligent mentor for the NBA D-League (National Basketball Association Development League), and made himself available as a mentor for young players who had the goal to play professionally.

Feeling God had a definite purpose for him, he sought opportunities to serve, but for the successful businessman, having to adjust the course was a part of that journey. Involved with high-end clients and corporations, and taking what he now feels was a sidetrack, God once again helped Derrick keep his earlier promise by granting him a wake-up call.

Derrick experienced a brain aneurism that could have ended his life.

Blessed to have no ill effects from the aneurism, Boles altered his course and disentangled from more worldly obligations to find ways to serve as originally planned. He feels as if God at that time was gently yet firmly saying, "Remember the promise you made when you were twenty-six? I gave you an international basketball opportunity. And now, I need you."

Boles' idea for the meaningful Stand Up journey across the United States was intended for celebrities and other athletes. Little by little as that plan fell through, he decided (in increments) to personally make that cycling trip.

While some might consider a trip across America a bucket list item, Boles was hesitant. He was not like the professional long-distance athletes he'd tried to outsource the ride to. Making the decision a matter of prayer, he came to understand that the journey has always been his to take.

"I had to do it," Derrick relates, "Who else was going to do it? The message to Stand Up, ranging from school bullying to community empowerment to social activism was so powerful. This had to get done."

Stand Up was created, hallmarked by an inspiring and eventful ride on two generously donated ElliptiGOs, and Boles now travels the world, bringing lessons of courage, compassion, character, critical thinking and common sense to schools, businesses, communities, and corporations. Boles believes that if he's not living in alignment with God's purpose for him, he won't be here.

He is grateful for each day he's able to spread the important message of Standing Up.

INTRODUCTION

LEADERSHIP HAS BEEN DISCUSSED AND DEBATED FOR HUNDREDS OF YEARS, WITH CONVERSATIONS CHALLENGING THEORIES ON THE IDEALS AND PROCESSES THAT WOULD HAVE THE HIGHEST IMPACT ON WHAT IT WOULD TAKE TO BECOME A TRULY INFLUENTIAL LEADER.

My leadership experience began at an early age.

In my preschool years in the United States, one of the first things I learned about was "alphabetical order". From A to Z, children were lined up according to the beginning letter of their last name. With the surname of "Boles", I quickly found there were not many children with last names that began with an "A", so each time we lined up, whether it was for school photos, lunch, or any formal school event, I was compelled to walk at the front of the line.

If not standing out enough already, I was also abnormally large. In the second grade I stood at five feet, one inch, and by age eight, I weighed 118 pounds. I didn't realize at the time that this would later be a gift, that it would one day mean an automatic number one draft pick when it came to sports and other activities during my youth. What it meant to me back then was that time and again, I was going to be called on to go first.

Leadership at such an early age can be a great teacher. I learned what it really took to mobilize and galvanize the individuals around me to form a collective group around a common vision.

As I attempted to fumble my way through adolescence, I was thankful for the best example of leadership I could have ever had, my mother, Norma Nell (Woods) Boles.

I'm not sure she knew how well she taught me, or of the sound framework for leadership that she provided through the way she lived her life.

Today's society is experiencing a void in leadership. There are still positions of leadership, and people fill them, yet many are discouraged with the current trends in leadership, so conversely, we don't have people willing to follow the leaders currently stepping up to the plate.

"Courage to Lead" is an effort to bring back the true essence of leadership and realign our moral compass. It examines how true leaders should conduct themselves, and explains the traits that make a person one worthy of following. As with my own mentors, you'll have certain words and phrases presented to you more than once. This is by design, since repetition is how people learn.

I've spent over thirty years in either leadership or leadership training positions, engaging in conversations with some of the world's great leaders of thought. This book is a combination of personal experience, research, and universal truths.

My hope is that you'll find the reading encouraging, thought provoking, and useful for developing yourself, and leaders of the next generation. I appreciate your concern for our future, and how that makes you a participant in the journey.

STEP ONE:

COURAGE

The five elements of Standing Up begin with courage, because everything else flows from it.

Courage is defined as the ability to do something that's frightening, the act of standing firm in the presence of some kind of personal pain or grief. It takes courage to stand up for the things you know to be right. It takes courage to become who you were meant to be.

Once you've developed your courage, so many other things in your life will fall into place. So if you feel your life is messed up right now, you know what's missing?

That's right.

It Doesn't Take Much

Hold up your little finger and stare at it for a minute. It only takes a pinky's worth of courage to make your own choices, and to stand up for yourself and those around you. Don't just sit there on the sidelines wishing you'd said something or done something. Get in the game.

Martin Luther King, Jr., said, "The time is always right to do the right thing."

You'll have no regrets to live with if you do the right thing. Martin Luther King, Jr. also said that we'll have to repent of this generation, not for the actions of the bad people, but for the "appalling silence of the good people."

Why are we being so silent?

Much of my silence was broken after my life was spared from a brain aneurism, but that wasn't the first time I was spared.

When I was growing up in Detroit, everyone had a nickname that had something to do with his or her personality or the way they were living their lives. One kid went by the nickname of "Peanut", because he was nuts, certifiably crazy. He fought teachers at school, threw bricks through glass windows, he was just a violent person.

What made Peanut tough wasn't necessarily him, it was his entourage. It's the same for most bullies, if you think about it, always having to run in packs because they aren't brave enough to stand on their own.

Peanut had an entourage of four or five guys that hung out with him and did whatever he said, and that made him appear to be larger than life.

I had some things going for me back then. I was big for my age, had the pretty eyes, and the girls liked me. I was viewed as the "good guy", while people thought of Peanut as the "bad guy".

And Peanut...he hated me for that.

When we were all in middle school, I had a crush on a girl named Shonta Langford. One weekend Shonta was throwing a birthday party over at her house, and I was invited. In Detroit, many of the houses had basements where the parties were held.

Peanut told everyone we knew that if I showed up in that basement for Shonta's party, he'd beat me down.

The news spread like wildfire.

Because I had a crush on Shonta, I had to go to that party. If I didn't, she'd think I was a punk. But if I went, I knew I was going to get beat down.

It would be my first big lesson in courage.

On the night of the party, I snuck into Shonta's basement, and was relieved to see that Peanut wasn't there.

Everything was going great until I saw Peanut and his boys coming down the stairs, and there was only one exit. My plan was to move around the perimeter of the room, try to get to Shonta to say "Happy Birthday", and then move the opposite direction of Peanut and the gang, working towards the stairway.

I finally reached Shonta, loved on her a little, told her "Happy Birthday", and then I was gone.

I remember thinking, "Everything's good," as I walked down the street towards my house, just as I heard the rush of the crowd gathering behind me. I turned around, and there was Peanut, his boys, and the entire party flooding out of Shonta's basement. They were all running in my direction, because there was going to be fight and they wanted to watch.

As the wave of people ran towards me in the dark at ten-thirty p.m., I knew a defining moment was coming, but I would not be the hero in this story.

Peanut threw the first punch, and his buddy Brian threw the second. Both hit me in a solid way. Tony was there with them, and they all began to beat me down. I dropped to the ground as they kicked and stomped. Then someone jumped onto my back, and I heard that person scream, "Stop, stop, stop!"

And they did, they stopped. Because a little, petite girl named Tawsha Robinson was sitting there on my back, crying, and saying, "What are you guys doing?"

Her question diffused everything. Killed it.

People in the crowd were affected too, and they started saying to Peanut and the boys, "What y'all doin', man?" as I'm down on the ground, crying.

Everyone turned on Peanut, Brian, and Tony, who suddenly felt ashamed. They said to each other, "Let's just go."

After those boys left, Tawsha walked with me to my house. I looked down at her and just shook my head. I hadn't been good friends with Tawsha, we didn't know each other that well; she was just someone I went to school with. But on that dark night in the Detroit street, the humanity in her said, "This is not going to happen. If you beat him down, you're going to have to beat me down, too."

It had nothing to do with her physical size, but everything to do with the size of her character.

I was amazed at the way she'd jumped on me during that fight. She was so small that the bulk of her only covered my torso, but her doing so had put an end to things.

As we walked, I promised myself I would never, ever be a coward again. If Tawsha could do it, so could I. I was six foot, five inches, three hundred pounds, and even though my friends called me the "gentle giant", I could have really hurt some people, but hadn't. It just wasn't in my DNA, although there were times after that incident where I had to live in that space.

I never wanted to be a fighter, and I believe that holds true for most people; that no one wants to be a thug or a killer. Anyone studying Abraham Maslow's "Hierarchy of Needs" regarding the theory of human motivation might understand what comes into play when people defend themselves or lash out at one another. We all want safety, esteem, and a sense of belonging. Our methods of getting those things are what make the difference.

Most people only become thugs and killers because they believe they have to be, thinking, "It's either going to be them, or it's going to be me."

What they don't realize is that they're me, and I'm them.

We're all connected.

Risk is An Element of Courage

Courage has a direct correlation to risk. Where courage is involved, there will always be something at stake.

When Tawsha Robinson jumped on my back to protect me, she was saying to Peanut and everyone else there that night, "If you want to get to him, you have to go through me."

We could use more of the Tawsha Robinson kind of nobility in our society, the type that says, "If you're going to burn him, you've got to burn me, too."

We are too into minding our own business, and we tell ourselves, "This doesn't involve you". Those are the lies that get told, but it's an apathetic mindset, another way to say, "Huh, that's messed up, I feel bad for them", and then do nothing.

If that same scene unfolded before us today, some kid that thought he was tough and his followers trying to beat some other kid down, would there be another Tawsha Robinson in the crowd?

Let's Get This Started

The biggest component to courage is that when you start something, you don't know how it's going to be received, or if you'll get any support. You just keep moving forward because you feel in your core that it's the right thing to do. The struggle seems larger if there's a massive amount of indecision, but what tips the scale is that the courageous person wants change far more than they want their so-called safety and comfort.

Everything good flows from courage, because its base is truth, and truth is the strongest thing there is. When your exert courage, you're taking that first step towards something better, and there's a benefit to that. Stepping out in courage defines your identity, and since much of society's problems stem from people not knowing who they are or what they believe in, courage neutralizes that. It's easy to get distracted in this life by the people and things that might want a say in who you are, but when you choose courage, you're first in line to have that say on who you want to be, and who you want to become.

Once you've chosen courage, get ready. You're going to become a person that others are drawn to, because your strength will get noticed. You'll be known for whom you are and what you stand for, and there's a residual effect. Tawsha Robinson had no idea what her standing up for me would help me to become, or what my standing up would help others to become. I can tell you, though, that from that moment on, I vowed that I would no longer tolerate, allow, or accept unwarranted and disrespectful behavior. Tawsha's courage helped me to build up my own.

Can you catch the vision of what would happen if we, and everyone around us, had the courage to become what we really are, and then stood together? There could very quickly be an entire network of leaders who'll "Stand Up" for moral decency within schools, and improve the climates there. Then, the students they influence will take those lessons home to their parents, who will convey what they're learning to their workplaces, extended families and beyond. Suddenly, we're all a part of the solution.

Our country has a division problem right now, and until that's remedied, things will continue to decline. Just think about it: we can all play a role in reversing that trend. If you're someone who is willing to step up and start leading, this world will be different because of you.

Your Turn

So who or what have you stood up for? What won't you tolerate anymore?

Denis Waitley said, "There are two primary choices in life: either accept conditions as they exist, or accept the responsibility for changing them."

If we expect any changes to occur, we need to start with ourselves. If we really believe what we say we believe, then we will be willing to lose everything.

I've met so many people who say, "Yep, I'm gonna, I'm gonna." But then...nothing. I don't judge them, but I know that internally they don't have the courage yet. There's this entire dormant population that appears to be indifferent, what the Bible calls "lukewarm". They're contemplating what might be lost if they were to stand up one day and say, "That's not right...that's not right."

Here's encouragement for those of you who are battling internally: I'm telling you to GO. DO.

There's momentum in this, and that momentum is a part of the indecision, because once you go, you can't go back, can't unsay it, can't undo it, and on some level, we all know that. It only takes a pinky's worth of courage to act, but once you do, the ball is rolling, and that's a good thing. We need those who are willing to give the ball that nudge in such a way that it's not coming back, creating a chain reaction that alters the makeup of things; changing everything in its path.

That's the kind of chemistry we're talking about; the kind where things are different because you did something that took some guts.

Don't Just Be a Fan

There are plenty who want to glob onto those who are strong without risking or sacrificing, and we call those "fans", but you don't want to be a fan and borrow on someone else's strength and light. You need to get your own strength and light, and here's the formula:

Risk plus sacrifice equals courage.

Courage requires putting something at stake, but many people don't want to put anything at stake. Not their reputations, not their livelihood, not their (often shallow) friendships.

On the other side of courage is strength.

You can always decide to skip the risk, to not get stronger, but remember that if you're not getting stronger, you're losing ground and becoming weaker.

Martin Luther King, Jr. said, "You died when you refused to stand up for Right, Truth, and Justice."

A part of you will die each time you go against yourself, and to me, that seems even riskier than standing up to do something. The faith you exhibit when standing up is the doorway to many more opportunities. When those opportunities are not taken, it depletes your faith account, where the balance is either growing or shrinking. Some choose not to grow their faith, and stay in the exact same place. But, when it's exercised, that faith grows, to the point that there might be complete chaos and madness all around you, but inside there is no fear.

Failure is Good

Part of being courageous involves not being afraid to fail. One of the best ways to bring about change is to try something new, but don't expect to be perfect at it when you're just starting out. Change is a trial and error process. Mistakes make wonderful teachers; they're some of the greatest educators of our time. They're not only one of the best ways to build character and endurance, they're an excellent tool for showing yourself how committed you are to whatever it is you're engaged in, so allow your failures to become teaching tools for how to move forward.

The God Factor

For me, God is a big part of my journey, my life, my family, and my vision of what I'm doing. He is ultimately where my courage comes from, and when you think of anyone in history that has been asked to lead, you'll realize that each of those people became empowered by the source that is God.

There is true power in being the sort of person who knows they've got "backup", and who doesn't change for those around them, or for the culture they've been dropped into. Those who maintain their sense of self, and who aren't worried about making everybody "comfortable" encourage others to be who they are, too. There will always be people whose feathers you'll ruffle when you step out in truth. So what. You can be that one person that isn't giving in to something as petty and false as peer pressure, and if you are, others will eventually follow. It just takes one, and you can't lead unless you go first.

The Courage to Be Who You Are

Courage also involves allowing your genius to show. Everyone has genius; ideas, concepts, maybe even relationships they should be following up on, but not everyone is brave enough to display that. When genius is acted upon, everyone benefits, because it's no longer about self, it's about being willing to step out of the comfort zone, realize untapped abilities, and become the confident human being you were meant to be, grabbing life with a new kind of vigor. When you do this, you'll give others the courage to do the same.

Faith and Humility Are Elements of Courage

Faith plays no small part in courage, and when it comes to faith, many still don't understand God's laws and principles. When you believe you can, that brings joy to God. It means you're willing to try something, even though you have no idea if it's going to work, even if you're not sure it can really happen, or how you're going to get there. When you're stepping out in faith, you act, and you just go. Stepping out allows God the opportunity to show up for you. When you're trying to do it all on your own, it's like saying to him, "No, I've got this", and he can't show up.

If you keep a humble attitude and acknowledge that you have no idea how it's all going to happen, but you're still willing to move forward, he can show up with help. That's the space you want to be living in.

Once you've got the courage part down and your perspective has expanded, your horizons are unlimited, because you'll be the kind of person that if called to go, will go in faith. With the strong combination of courage, faith, humility, and a willing mind, you'll be continually presented with opportunities. You'll be someone that others will count on to speak out against the evil you see in the world, and at that point you'll be involved in changing the culture into something that you choose, instead of being dictated by culture.

Truth

Courage is the action and the vessel that conveys TRUTH.

If you ever want to be someone that makes an impact in this life, speak truth and love (really one and the same), and you'll be unstoppable. When truth is conveyed, you're going to have extra help, no matter what forces are fighting against you.

If you speak out in truth, it doesn't matter how jumbled the message, or how much the actual content might lack, people will still be drawn to what you're saying. Because truth is felt. People can feel love, and they can feel truth churning inside of them. They'll think, "I don't know what it is, but there's just something about that person, I think I need to get to know them better."

Here's some truth: many people think it's uncomfortable to talk about racism. I think it's far more uncomfortable to say nothing and have to live with it.

I was at an in-service meeting in the heart of Idaho when one lady approached me and said, "When I heard you were coming, I was so excited. Did they fly you in?"

I tried to suppress a grin, and told her that no, I actually lived in Idaho.

She was shocked.

"You...live...here?" she said, then went on, "Oh, my gosh, all the stuff you do all over the United States. I thought you lived in, like, Dallas."

Here's some more truth: Why is it that we're downplaying ourselves? Why can't something good like a movement to Stand Up come from our home state, or our hometown?

That's another lesson about truth. No one has the corner on it; it can be found anywhere, so don't limit yourself because you think it ought to come from a certain type of person, place, or area.

Truth is magnetic. People, whether they realize it or not, are drawn to it. So once you start speaking truth, be ready. It's what the human race craves.

Truth is something that's always been my gift, but I'm not alone in that. We were all born with a God given gift for cleaving to and speaking the truth, but not all of us use it. When we tap into that birthright, things in our lives begin to change. We become more than we were. Truth expands people.

If you're ever confused about what truth is and what it isn't, think about this: Does what was said or done linger in your mind, not fade out? That's one clue that you're dealing with truth.

Another clue: do things occur to back those words up? Is there noticeable, good fruit from those words or deeds? That's another surefire way you can know that what you have heard, or read, or felt was the truth.

Humor is a large percentage of truth. When someone tells it like it is, it's often funny, because most of the time everyone's thinking it, but not everyone's saying it. There's a lot of talk out there, but not the kind of talk that should be happening. Not enough people are speaking out like they should, and it's very interesting. They're all dancing around the same concepts with their words, but aren't getting to the heart of it, so none of it is truth; it's just watered down, politically correct stuff.

Although everything I'm saying to you right now might not be mind-boggling or ground-breaking, if it sticks around in your head, if you see some changes happening in your life because of what you have heard or felt, guess what? That's truth right there. Because truth is two things: it's simple, and it lasts.

If you're thinking about it next month, then it's probably the truth.

The courage to stand up for truth and what is right, stand up for others, and to stand up and be who you really are is the wellspring of all other aspects of the Stand Up program.

Let's Talk

➢ Have you had times in the past when you didn't stand up and exercise that "pinky's worth" of courage? If you didn't say and do what your conscience prompted you to at the time, what were the after effects?

➢ Think of a time when you DID stand up, how did that make you feel?

➢ Do you know someone (of any age) who has to "run with the pack" to appear stronger than they actually are?

➢ What are the differences between "Peanut" and Tawsha Robinson?

➢ Do you have a few people in your life like Tawsha Robinson who you know would say, "If you want to get to them, you'll have to go through me" and really mean it? Who are they?

➢ What sorts of things are going on in your world right now that could use someone with courage to resolve? What would it look like if that happened?

➢ What is the formula for courage?

➢ Why does it require courage to show who you really are? What areas in your life could you use courage to display more of who you are?

➢ What are the two things that compile truth?

STEP TWO:

COMPASSION

It doesn't matter where you go; the need for compassion is exactly the same all around the world.

Not too long ago, I was in Sydney, Australia with some pretty high-level corporate people. I'd just done a few seminars for them, and they were taking me to dinner at a nice restaurant downtown. We walked through the heart of Sydney, all well-dressed and looking good.

And then it happened; our group approached a man on the sidewalk that appeared to have rolled in filth, his face and clothing looked that dirty. He talked to himself in sort of a shouting way, loud and belligerent. I think the consensus was that he'd been drinking.

There were plenty of divisions between our group and that man. We were dressed for a night at an expensive restaurant downtown, had spent time preparing, smelled nice, all of it, and he looked like a homeless person. This was the assessment we were buying into. We also bought into our being, you know, whoever we thought we were. We didn't want to get "infected" with whatever it was that man might have had.

The group of successful executives moved over to the other side of the walkway in order to avoid him, and I'm sure most of us were thinking, "He's drunk, he's on drugs, he's mentally unstable, and we need to steer clear."

His words were coming out in random phrases, it was shocking, and impossible to ignore at that volume.

In my spirit, I knew that moving to the other side was not what we should be doing. As we got closer to where he was, I became more and more drawn to this person. While the others were practically up against the wall to avoid an encounter, I turned towards the man, and he and I approached each other. Some in the group turned around, but didn't say anything. They acted slightly in awe of what was about to happen.

The man and I just connected. I gave him a hug for five or six seconds, he in his filth, and me in my nice, go-to-dinner-downtown clothing. I felt impressed to tell him that I loved him, and that God loved him, and when I did that, he stared at me and said, "What did you just say?"

He'd stopped what he was doing. The belligerence, the volume, it all just stopped. Our interaction brought him back to earth.

I repeated, "I love you, and I want you to know that God loves you."

He replied, "Man...I don't know why you told me that, but that's exactly what I needed to hear. Thank you."

Maybe all that man had wanted was love. Babies cry out when they need something; perhaps when the pain gets to be acute enough, adults are no different. I wondered, how bad off does a person need to be in order to get to the point that they're literally yelling for attention? How many bouts of pure loneliness and pain did he have to endure before getting to that point? Considering that most of us are conditioned not to yell unless it's an "emergency", my guess is that he was pretty desperate. So much so that his mindset was, "All right, I don't know what else to do, so I'm just going to walk down the street and yell. Maybe somebody will finally hear me."

More than anything, maybe that man just needed to know that somebody cared, that he mattered.

As I walked away after our exchange, there was no more angry noise. It was as if peace had descended on that street, and a feeling of calm blanketed over everything. I looked back, and the man was still standing there, visibly shaken, as if asking himself, "Okay, what just happened?"

Then he went on his way, and I went on mine. I didn't even know the man, but that didn't matter. His face is permanently etched on my mind, and I'm pretty sure my face is etched on his.

There's more.

Even though the people I was with all smelled good, I'd rushed out the door without putting on any cologne that night. I just had a "blah" essence to me. You can only imagine how one might smell after hugging a man who looked like he was homeless, who seemed that dirty. But after I hugged that man and walked away, it occurred to me that he had actually smelled really good. And now, I smelled like him, and I smelled great. I have no idea what that man was wearing, there's no way to explain it. He was dirty, his clothes were dirty, and yet I smelled that good.

If we're dealing with people that we feel are "different" from us, a lot of the time we worry that we're going to a "get a little on us". And I did, but not in the way I expected.

My Greatest Mentor of Compassion

When you're on a plane for fourteen hours in one stretch, you have a lot of time to think. On one such flight, my mom kept appearing in my mind.

I thought about everything I saw her do while I was growing up. We lived on the back side of I-94 West that led into Detroit. Our home was only twenty-five feet or so away from the expressway, and cars would break down nearby twenty-four hours a day. There were many houses crowded together in our neighborhood, yet of all the houses to go to, we somehow attracted every family in distress.

I remember one of the first times that happened, on a night when we were just sitting down to dinner. We heard a knock at our back door, which was unusual because people came to our front door in normal situations.

"Who on earth could be knocking at our back door?" said my mom, who often expressed her thoughts out loud.

She opened the door to find a young mother and four children standing outside. I don't know what the exchange was between them at that back door, but I do know that my mother was a strong and discerning woman. If she invited a complete stranger and her four children into our home, she felt in her heart that was the right thing to do at the time. I didn't mind, it meant I'd have some new friends to play with, and we played together for hours, and shared our dinner with them, too.

While I was playing, I noticed that my mother took the time to listen to this young woman who'd so unexpectedly chosen our home as a refuge. My mother engaged with her as she talked about her struggles, with the sincere intent to understand. Even at my young age, I noticed the process unfolding, and recognized that my mother was creating a calm and stable environment for people she had no knowledge of or history with. I watched as she slowly built trust and respect between herself and the young woman, how she tried to comprehend both her situation and disposition.

I watched similar scenes unfold repeatedly as random people began to knock on our back door, having jumped the fence to get to our house, of all the houses on the block, because they "just had a feeling about the place."

These people were caught in emergency situations, and that's when a true leader is at their best. It's when leaders are most relevant, and most needed. The compassion lessons my mother taught me by helping those people had a profound impact years later on myself and the people I came to mentor and coach.

Our family was from Tuscaloosa, Alabama, and my mother moved not just our family to Detroit (where there was far more freedom, opportunity, and, it seemed, far less discrimination), but our extended family, too.

Once we were settled in a city like Detroit that was on the cusp of a new age, she continued to move family members up from the South. None of them had any money or much of anything, and they'd stay with us for anywhere from six months to a year. Not only did they stay with us, we fed them, too. When they got on their feet, they'd move to their own apartment, and then my mother would take on somebody else.

As a kid, I watched her do that four or five times, and frequently thought to myself in a resigned way, "Huh. Okay..." That kind of example of service was shown me throughout my childhood, and as a young man growing up, I learned the importance of compassion as a big part of leadership development.

My mother built a community, and I'm not just talking about a bunch of people sitting around a dinner table. I'm talking about families getting on their feet so they could go out and help others. There were these huge ripples, and I watched and learned from my mother that good and effective leaders are those who understand the position, circumstances, and mindset of the people they're serving. In a world where the word "compassion" isn't frequently used in leadership, for my mother, that word was a cornerstone.

Her relatives would tell her, "Auntie, we love you, you're unbelievable."

As an adult, I think back to all she did, and ask myself, "Who was she?"

I didn't understand back then what I was witnessing. I just knew that, all right, my cousins were moving from Alabama, and that Mom said there would soon be two extra people in my room. And once they moved out, there would be more.

There was an element of fear for me, too. I knew of our lack of resources, and thought surely we'd be living in a totally different space soon. But that never happened.

Just like with the man on the street in Australia, I thought we'd "get dirty" or "catch something" from the way we were helping. I expected the worst; to lose our home and to not have enough food to eat. A lot of the time when we think about giving like that, we think we're going to lose, but for us, that didn't occur.

We came off smelling good.

Rewards of a Different Kind

Someone asked me once if my mother was ever repaid for her kindness, if anyone came back to our home with several bags of groceries, or slipped her a few twenty-dollar bills as a "thank you".

I'm not aware of that ever happening. But my mother wasn't looking for that. I used to feel bad for my mom, because I felt like she didn't get those rewards she so richly deserved, but maybe she did. I think her relationship with God was so profound that her strength, spirit, and her leadership within our family reflected that relationship profoundly. The woman sacrificed tons. Tons. And the reward for that was that she was strong enough to help others. She was also surrounded by a tribe of her own making, full of people that would have gone to war for her. She felt needed, she felt important, she felt loved, and she felt that she belonged.

My mother showed us that she loved us, and then she showed us that she loved other people. We knew this to be true because of the things we witnessed her doing and saying.

She told me that she loved me, she told others, and now I'm a grown man who can say the same thing to total strangers, no matter who they are or what they look like. So maybe my mother did get her reward after all, just not in the conventional way we might think.

When someone needed help, it didn't matter to my mother who they were, she was going to help them, but not everyone thinks that way. If we're talking about rewards, let me explain another payoff for my mother's type of mindset.

If you grew up with judgment, criticism, with things needing to be just so, that will take some work to overcome. You might ask, if you're in that corner, how you can get out of that habit of the mind. It might sound overly simplistic to just say, "Don't judge them," but here's the motivator:

When your brain is in that rut, you're not happy. And when you're in that space, you are blocking the blessings and miracles that are all around you.

Those businessmen in Sydney stopped walking when I approached that man that was shouting in the street, and they watched in what almost seemed like awe, as if they couldn't understand it. But I wasn't doing anything that wasn't available to them, too. I really wasn't. All I was doing was to love a person without judgment, without ego.

That's what creates those miracles. That's the kind of behavior that starts to change things.

If you're in that rut, you're closing down your own joy and blessings and don't even know it. You're so busy worrying about if something makes sense, or whether it's going to positively affect the bottom line. If the answer to that is "no", many won't do it.

Aren't you tired of being in a rut? Isn't it getting boring?

There are positive ways to "live dangerously" and "take risks". They come from Standing Up and saying yes to blessings and miracles.

And when you do, you're going to come off smelling good.

It's Always a Two Way Street

Don't underestimate the power of being open to people. When you're closed, others can see it from your body language, because everything closes up. Eyes narrow, shoulders hunch, arms and legs cross, fists clench. Everything about feeling that way is unhealthy and uncomfortable.

There is magic in opening up to people. When I've talked to groups of 300 or more, I take the time to shake everyone's hand. If you ever get the opportunity to do something like that, you'll quickly come to the conclusion that this isn't about you. You're just the one bringing the message of love, and of the change that's coming, but in the meantime, you're going to get thanked. You'll be told you're a "good dude" or a "good bloke" or whatever, and it's important to hear that.

But the message of love and acceptance I'm delivering isn't just for them, either. Most of the time when I'm in front of people feeling passionate about what I'm telling them about, I'm talking to myself. You might be receiving it, but I have to get around the lessons, too. While I'm speaking, I'm sharpening my own tools, perfecting my own self.

We're Talking to Ourselves

It's not the just the man on the street who is shouting. In one way or another, we're all shouting for attention, we all want to know that we matter.

Everywhere we look, people are shouting, hurting. Not long ago we had protests at the capital in Idaho, right downtown. There were people stopping cars, protesting unfair treatment, and reiterating that black lives matter.

If we really stop to look at the way we've been treating one another, it's no small wonder. Even with our language, we can be so calloused. Take that phrase, "the race card", someone's "pulling the race card".

Let me see if I can put that into context. Say there's a young lady who suffered a brutal sexual assault, and that event now pervades her entire life. If she displays that she's affected in some way, and is continually talking about it, what if one day when she mentions it again, someone says, "Oh, sure, pull out your rape card."

How utterly insensitive is that? How do you think that young lady would feel when someone tries to trivialize that she's been through?

The truth is that everybody's got their card. Abuse, divorce, addiction, underprivileged, and the list can go on and on. So, we have to be careful, because those are all very real things. That stuff really does happen to people. Slavery happened. Rape happened. Abuse happened.

Many of us just want to go, yeah, yeah, but we didn't do it. It wasn't my grandparents that put you into slavery or mistreated you, so can we just move forward?

I get that, but the entire problem is that it hasn't been acknowledged, and until it is, it's not going away. Just like that guy on the street, it's only going to get louder.

Those people who are hurting want to be told, "I hear you, I love you."

But who's going to say it? Who's it going to be? Do people think the government's going to fix this, because they can't. It's not going to be the government that finally makes our social structure one that's healed.

Last Saturday they had a million person march on Washington, D.C. in the United States. I assure you, this isn't going away. Empathy and compassion are what can start that healing process, but who is that going to come from?

Here we are, all of us raising our voices, but to whom are we really raising our voices? The political system? Society? Each other?

Consider that we are raising our voices to ourselves.

And it won't go away till we fix it.

Fixing What's Broken

So how do we fix the billions of broken hearts out there that want their voices heard? The answer lies in chemistry. Something has to change in the chemistry in order to start a chain reaction that allows others to start self-healing. In order to do that, something has to alter the atmosphere, or something has to be added from outside of a situation or individual, in order for self-healing to take place and continue to do so.

In my world, I call that a catalyst.

Catalysts for Compassion

Catalysts are people or things that change circumstances. They are put into lives to change lives, and everyone has them, but not everyone sees them. The same moment you're aware of the catalysts in your life, that's when you're going to believe you're loved. Because God wouldn't bother to put a catalyst into your life unless he loved you and had compassion for you.

My mom is a catalyst. The other day in Australia, I was able to be a catalyst for the man on the street, and he was a catalyst for me.

Dale Brown, my mentor and Shaquille O' Neal's coach at Louisiana State University, is a catalyst, the first man to ever tell me he loved me, and that altered my life. When Dale Brown was a senior in high school, he heard he was loved from a tough coach. Dale Brown had sworn at one of the Catholic nuns at his school on that day, and the coach threw Dale up against the lockers, threatened him, and then ended with, "I love you, Dale Brown."

Coach Brown has now said "I love you" to countless other young men he's mentored, and I was one of them. Now I'm saying it to you, and it's the truth.

We all have the potential to become catalysts in this world, starting with ourselves. Tonight before you go to bed, and then again tomorrow morning when you get up, look at yourself in the mirror and say three times out loud, "I believe", and mean it. This is magic. You try that, and just see what occurs.

Big things happen when you start liking, and then loving yourself. Once you do, you can start loving on others, and the impact of that will be world changing.

I get it. These days it's hard to know what love is anymore. So I'll tell you what it isn't: It isn't a lot of talk. Love is an ACTION, not a discussion. Love is something someone does. Love involves helping, encouraging, being there.

There's a huge need in the world these days for people to love. Just look around. Someone you'll encounter today is in darkness, guaranteed. Did you ever think that YOU could be that light for them? It doesn't matter who it is, that love is needed. I can tell you that I've been to so many A-list events, and they're all just people. Not only are they all just people, some of them, a lot of them, are broken. They're broken because we've worshiped them and turned them into our idols, when they're really only people like us, and some of them need our help.

Look around again. Every single person in your view has the potential to become something great. YOU have the potential to become something great, and you become great by helping others grow into what they can be. By first believing in you, and then believing in them. It doesn't matter who you are or where you've been; it is never too early or too late to make an impact on someone else's life, starting with your own.

Who Have You Stood Up For?

So, I'm going to ask you this: Who have you stood up for recently?

Standing up for someone is a big part of love and compassion.

No matter the age, all of us are dealing with the daily pressures of fitting in. Everyone needs approval from their current or potential friends, and that can result in being too afraid to say "no" when it needs to be said, which can lead to some problems.

Children especially have a barrage of these types of pressures. Gangs, drugs and alcohol, bullying, violence, discrimination, and the current day leadership crisis can get to be too much for even the sanest of adults to handle, let alone someone who has a young, developing mind.

Add to that the integration to the new norms, the technology, and the sitcoms on television. Those things are going to create negative, generational impacts to our country on detrimental levels. From a social and humanities perspective, many of our youth are ill equipped, and that's our fault. We haven't been paying attention.

People are getting cyber bullied and committing suicide. Those doing the cyber bullying don't comprehend the potential outcomes, because they don't have the face-to-face interaction, and consequentially lack the emotional tools people once had. Connectivity is no longer as well understood, and many leaders aren't pushing for that.

Educators work diligently to fill young minds with the required information to move onto the next grade or graduate to higher education, but what is being done to educate and prepare individuals for what is within and outside of their own school walls? Just how far a person goes in life will depend upon how tender they were with the young, how compassionate they were with the aged, how sympathetic with the striving, and how tolerant they were of both the weak and the strong, because at some point in their lives, they will have been all of those things.

We might think a lack of caring won't matter, but someday, that's going to be us. For a youth, that's hard to wrap the head around. They haven't had those experiences yet, but they will, it's coming. We see horrible things happening in other parts of the country, and think, "bummer for them", but those things could so easily be happening on our own streets. We should instead be thinking, okay, what could we do to help, to make this better? Because, after all, those people we're watching on TV? That could be us.

How it's Supposed to Work

I really think we've forgotten how it's all supposed to work.

We're raising children that are distracted by games, TV, the Internet, and the adults in their lives are distracted, too. The underlying message for both adults and children is, "I don't care about you." Then, we unconsciously convey that message to everybody else. "You don't care about me, so I don't care about you."

It's not hard to see where suicides, murders, and all forms of abuse or self-abuse stem from. Nobody cares, so why should we? That equates to a real lack of value when it comes to human life.

What's happening is an epidemic, and we need to put a stop to it. Loving people is our responsibility as human beings.

For all of the reasons just listed, the number one goal is to bring people together.

The Invisible Enemy

Prejudice, the opposite of people being united, exists in our world today in all forms. At times it might be invisible to the eye, but that doesn't make it any less real. There's a spirit around prejudice that's almost tangible, and it's not limited to race. Prejudice can include age, size, social standing, financial standing, education; there's no limit to why one person might exclude another person from their friendship. Just think of the way you feel when someone gives you a dirty look for no understandable reason at all. This happens in communities, in schools, in homes, and it's filled with an incredibly destructive power.

The good news is that people can be developed, and those willing to step out and stand up will be equipped with what they need. I didn't have what I needed when starting my ride across America. I'm no distance athlete. But I had what I needed (strength, endurance, patience) when I got to the other side.

With the right kind of leadership, lives can be renewed, courses can be corrected, and prejudices can be put aside. I want to open that conversation, and ask you to join me in tapping into the vast potential that's already there. Let's draw it out.

Leading with Love

When it comes to good leadership, compassion is a big part of that. The only way for leaders to be effective is to have a discernment of those they're leading, and to be the type of leader who isn't willing to sacrifice those followers, just because they know those people might follow them blindly into battle. Any follower that's being treated like a mere cog in the wheel can know with assurance they're following the wrong person, and if they continue to follow they'll find themselves closing up, going underground. When a leader has compassion and views all who choose to follow them as unique and precious, those within their stewardship bloom. No one is their best in any environment where they feel no value, and they won't be able to hear any leader's voice past the kind of mental noise that creates. A good, compassionate leader is an active part of a person's development. If you're with a leader who stifles you and couldn't care less, you've got to get out of that. You should not be following that person.

Start by Saying the Words

I'm here because I love people. That's the first thing I tell the students I speak to, and that's the first thing you should convey to anyone you want to lift. "The reason I'm here is because I love you."

This is what I tell the kids, and it's true. I once was them, and still am like them. When I see those kids, I see my daughter and my son. The moment I tell them "I love you", I get looks and stares and glares of all kinds. They simply don't know how to take it, because plenty of people have said those same words to them but haven't backed them up, so they're just words. I've been doing this for years now, and I can attest to this: Telling someone you love him or her and then backing it up with action is a game-changer. It's been shared with me that after I've visited schools, said what I've said, and did what I did, those schools are different. All I've done was plant the seeds.

At the very heart of things, the whole prejudice, black and white or race issue is not really what we're battling. We flesh-and-blood humans like to have everything so simple, so clean, but it's not like that. What we're battling right now are principalities of darkness and spiritual realms. And if we're not living with a clear intention, we're going to get caught up and distracted.

Too many people getting caught up is going to create the wrong kind of catalyst within our society, and that's what this is all building up to become, if we're not living with intention. You and I know things have been brewing for a while, but we choose not to see it. That's a dangerous way to live, and a reckless decision, because we don't know which straw will be the one to break the camel's back.

There's an undercurrent in communities, with entire groups of people stating that treatment towards them has been unfair, unequal. A person can only live in that space for so long, though, before asking themselves, "Okay, who am I, really? Am I going to live my life like this, or am I going to be willing to look for different opportunities, a different kind of life?"

If lives aren't lived with intention, history continues to repeat itself. That is, simply put, exactly how we got here.

So a person sees that they have potential, and then feels the desire to change. What that person needs to know is that they will not be doing the growing and changing alone, though at times it might feel like it. A common thread of love and humanity does exist, and it connects us. I can't tell you how many times throughout my life different individuals showed up that were inspired to do so. I can honestly say that if you really take a look around, you'll know you're not alone. There will be at least one good person in your life that if you let yourself, you can go to.

Global Examples

On a global level, we've seen excellent examples of this, from Gandhi to Mother Theresa to Martin Luther King, and what I marvel at was their pain quotient. Imagine all they've seen, how much emotional pain they've endured, the anguish over those around them that were hurting. I think of Nelson Mandela and the mental, emotional, physical, and spiritual pain he went through at the hands of his captors and torturers in prison. Yet, he worked hard to gain the mind-boggling power to forgive them, and to love them.

Every one of those people had a pain quotient. Every one of them had this mindset that said, "Even if you don't like me, even if you're trying to kill me, I've chosen beforehand that no matter what, I'm going to love you."

Many of those individuals also knew that a part of that love involved separating the behavior from the individual. They understood that some of the dark things people did were not a true representation of who they were. They had a strong, almost superhuman faith, and a relationship with something larger than themselves. That is the only way a mere human could internalize that and not lose their mind and heart to that kind of darkness. During an ongoing warfare of souls, managing to maintain love and compassion is difficult-to-impossible if that soul is tainted with vengeful, resentful thoughts. Being able to keep your soul filled up is a challenge, when so many of us are already running on 'E'.

But we can help each other. Those people I mentioned were all determined to love, relied on a higher power to help them do so, and that determination changed the world around them. Someone told Coach Dale Brown as a teenager that he was loved, he told me, and now I'm telling that to you, and encouraging you to pass that on, so you see how a simple act of love can be so enduring.

Our Responsibility

This is the number one thing: Loving people is our responsibility as human beings. Our ability to make the choice to love is what sets us apart from all other species.

When I was riding the ElliptiGO through Texas, just getting ready to cross the border into Louisiana, a 65-year-old grandmother and her grandson spotted me on the side of the highway. She rolled down her window to ask me what kind of unique bicycle I was on, why I was riding, and where I was going. When she found out what I was doing, she asked me to stop at an upcoming fast food restaurant so that she could buy my lunch, and said, "Whatever you want, you can have". During lunch, she encouraged her grandson to really listen to what I had to say. There we were at a fast food restaurant out in the middle of nowhere, becoming friends for life. We even took a picture of us, standing all together.

I thought about why that grandmother and others had been so open to helping me throughout my life's journey, and came up with what I feel is a common denominator: It seems that the older and / or wiser some people become, the less resistant they are to being compassionate. I think it has to do with experiencing a personal loss of some sort, or of being extremely aware of his or her own mortality. The reality of death makes people look at things differently; makes them less prone to being judgmental, less willing to follow the "script". It causes people to exude a mutual love for others, even if they don't know them.

Everyone Will Learn the Mortality Lesson

My mortality lesson was taught to me just a few years ago, and it changed everything. I woke up one night with what I thought was a bloody nose. In actuality, it was an aneurism, where an artery in the brain bulges, or, in my case, bursts. Most of the time when aneurisms occur in people, there are no symptoms. Depending on how it all goes down, an aneurism can lead to brain damage, a stroke, or death. Because of the severe nosebleed, I knew something was wrong.

That was my wake up call, and if you haven't had one of your own yet, it's coming.

Everyone Has Someone

In our fast-paced society with its microwave mentality, we've cut out compassion, that huge, vital piece of humanity, or it's just been blocked altogether. There's that message again, "You don't care about me, and so I don't care about you." But that's a lie. Whether you're aware of it or not, everyone has someone that cares about them.

Loving people is nature's way, and people don't have to be physically beautiful to deserve love. Beauty is defined by how we treat others and ourselves; it's a state of mind. Beauty is fulfilling your God-given purpose in standing up and inspiring others to know that they can be beautiful, too.

You look at the earth's relationship with animals and flowers, what lessons we can learn there. When it's cold and dark animals hibernate, flowers go underground. Things are dormant. But when there's the beginning of warmth and light, everything changes.

Be Open

There are days where I get a lot of messages on my voicemail. A while back, I was going through a cluster of them when one from a woman named Melissa who had just lost her teenage daughter days earlier to suicide made me hit the pause button. I could hear the sadness and hurt in her voice.

I myself had been going through something painful, was upset and in a good deal of despair and disappointment, and that had been creating a fog when it came to my mission. I hadn't taken any calls for the past two days, but Melissa's very heavy message made me stop. She'd called me out of the blue, having heard about what I was doing with the Stand Up movement. I listened to that message again, and was compelled to call her back.

This woman was distraught. For the next two hours, we talked, cried, and prayed together. Melissa had this heart-to-heart conversation with someone she'd never met before. She told me about her daughter's bullying and other problems that her family had been facing, and during that conversation we became like brother and sister.

Look at how fast total strangers can connect. That's the speed of trust and the speed of love. Why did that happen? Maybe because she'd just lost her daughter and was no longer following the "script".

When people realize how important we are to each other, it's because we get this fact: I am you, and you are me. At my age, I know now that I could have judged someone twenty years ago, and these days wind up in those exact same shoes. Whatever happens to you will, one day, be happening to me. Those who understand mortality or have had a loss get this. Is that what it will take to get the rest of us to that point, or can we learn that lesson without it?

After I hung up with Melissa, I sat for a moment, thinking, "That's what it is, that's what this is all about". It's about caring and being there, walking beside someone else.

Coming Alongside

Coming alongside of someone differs from having someone look to you as a leader, or following along. When you come alongside, you join people in their pain and grief. Melissa might have needed that phone call more than anyone will ever know; I think that's why I was prompted to call her back.

Again, I'll tell you this: a soul-to-soul connection can be made within an instant.

Being in a place of peace where you just love people is where you want to be, even though people are going to make mistakes, act like idiots, and say thoughtless things. Your choice to respond with love will bless your life.

How did people like Mother Theresa and Nelson Mandela keep going, how did they come alongside of so many others? I got a clue to that when I hung up the phone with that grieving mother, Melissa. Even though I was prompted to call her, the reality is that her strength and transparency filled my tank back up. By the time we'd said goodbye, she had actually helped me. Compassion is a two-way street.

The common thread of love and humanity exists, and is especially apparent when we truly come alongside of someone on their journey.

Choose Wisely Who to Come Alongside Of

Okay, so you have compassion. Does that mean you need to come alongside of everyone? Not necessarily. There are those that you love, want the best for, but that you cannot be around. It's not that you don't love them. You simply cannot be around them.

I have people that I love back in Detroit. Man, I love them. Love them. I want the best for them; I pray for them, I hope they'll find success with the things they're striving for. But I can't be around them, because doing that holds for me the very real possibility of getting killed. It could taint the work that I've done, and could potentially undermine the longevity of the Stand Up movement. I'm not saying these things to be mean, I'm saying these things because it's the truth. To achieve what I need to achieve means not being around certain individuals. That's not saying I'm any better than them. I'm just saying I'm in a different place, and that I have to keep moving. If my friends in Detroit can't help me with that, I have to move on, but I still love them.

There will be people in your life that you love, but that you can't be around, too. Compassion is the antidote for that. You can still care about them, and you can still find ways to help them, even if it's just keeping them in your prayers. You don't have to get close to everyone, people can be loved from a distance, but they still need to be loved. People deserve to be loved just because they exist, because they're alive, and that alone is precious.

Take a Second Look at the "Rules"

On the flipside, you don't want to be too closed. People sometimes miss opportunities because society has everything so scripted out on how friendships are supposed to go. Instant friendship isn't supposed to just happen, right? Society suggests that you don't just call someone and open up, there's a process. First you need be introduced, meet them at a networking meeting, or go have coffee or whatever. So much is scripted for us that we miss out on those powerful, life-changing moments, all because we're "supposed" to do things a certain way.

Part of compassion is not following those rules about how you're supposed to react if someone runs into your car, or steals your cell phone, or cuts in front of you in line. Our minds have been programmed for just such incidents, instead of halting that learned, kneejerk reaction and using our own judgment enough to say, "Hey, wait a minute. I don't have to do that. I'm going to choose to love this person."

I could call that mother, Melissa, right now, and not only would she take that call, I know she'd be happy to talk to me. She and I are now friends for life, because that "script" was tossed out. When someone lets you into his or her heart, it's a privilege, a sacred trust. Why would we not want that?

My good friend Ron has often gone to speaking engagements with me. I met him at a Business Days seminar. During that seminar I met a lot of people, and each gave me their business card, but there was something special about Ron. I called him when I didn't call anyone else. I felt for some reason like we needed to walk beside each other. People think we've been friends for twenty years, but it was the exact same thing as with Melissa.

By all assessments, Ron is a very successful businessman. He knew nothing about me, other than to hear me speak for a while at Business Days. I have to be honest and mention that in Idaho where I live, for someone like me, it's been hard to find high-level friendships that have no prejudice, but not with Ron, who retired at a young age and now spends his days serving others. Ron told me that even five years ago, he wouldn't have been involved in the things he's doing now. Ron wasn't following the script. His shift involved mortality, too. Losing his mother, whose biggest thing was the Golden Rule, was a traumatic and impactful event, and it changed him. He's now taking on her main theme of doing unto others as you would have them do unto you, and that's affecting a lot of people's lives, which is powerful.

Those intertwining wires exist, but if we're all listening to that same tired song of how things are "supposed" to be, our paths won't cross, and we'll just keep journeying alone.

So we put up these shells for "protection", but I'm now telling you to be vulnerable, open, and transparent. If that sounds like a lot, let me tell you this: you can do that as instantly as you can hate.

Hating is the Weaker Person's Way

Hating takes no effort at all. That's why so many people do it. There's little to no action required, not much thought behind it. The masses get to stay right where they are, or even backslide, and it takes nothing. While love is an action, you can hate without having to do a thing. It can be as simple as a look you give, or never speaking to a person.

Love takes effort, and it's the true sign of someone who has courage, because it takes courage to be vulnerable. It takes courage to get on the phone with someone you've never met and to cry and pray with him or her. You think courage means maintaining that image of a tough guy? No, no, no. Courage is being real and authentic, who you really are. It's putting up that wall, that façade that really hurts a person. And when people see that wall of yours, the message is, "I don't care about you", and then they think, "If you don't care about me, why should I care about you?"

Then the whole cycle starts all over again. Courage and compassion break down those walls.

Love does take effort, it requires you to take action, but anything powerful is worth the effort. If you love somebody, you have to back that up with action, but if you hate somebody, you won't have to do a thing. Going along with the herd shows no strength, no effort. Hate is the weaker person's way.

Empathy for You is Empathy for Me

My wife and I were watching the news yesterday, getting pretty emotional over the story of a local woman, a former bus driver that took part in an accident that resulted in the death of a twelve-year-old student. The woman's heart was broken over it all. If playing that same old song, some might think, "too bad for you, that's messed up", and "I'm glad it's not me". But that gets us nowhere. Something's got to change in our thinking; we've got to make a different decision. Our society cannot continue to wield such a sharp sword. None of us are perfect. We need to realize that that person is us. That person is US.

The Reason

Implant this in your mind: Anyone we might judge, ridicule, or fight against is us.

That's why we need to stand up and fight for things like treating people with respect, peace within the home, stronger relationships.

God works through people. We're His vessels. When we have our own walls up and are surrounded by darkness, he sends some random person. If we're following the "script", or if we're in hatred or anger when he sends that one person to comfort us, we might think (or even say), "What…you?"

That one person is here to come alongside of you, to love you unconditionally, and with no expectations. That's what compassion is.

NOTES

Let's Talk

➤ What were the words that stopped the man on the street in Australia from shouting? How would hearing those same words affect you?

➤ Who are the people in your life you might be avoiding, for fear you'll "get a little on you"?

➤ What did my mother do for the young mother that came to her door for assistance? What might that sort of treatment do for you during a crisis situation in your life?

➤ When are true leaders at their best?

➤ What did my mother do to build a community?

➤ When any of us are "shouting" for understanding, who are we really talking to?

➤ Who are the catalysts in your life?

➤ What is the phrase the Coach Dale Brown said to me that made such a difference? Who said that to Coach Dale Brown? Who do you know that could really use those words?

➤ What has to happen before you can start "loving on" others?

➤ Who has been an example of compassion in your life?

➤ What experiences might you have missed out on by following the "script"?

➤ Have you learned the "mortality lesson" yet? What instances taught you to value human life?

➤ How fast can a soul-to-soul connection be made?

➤ Are there people in your life that you should not be spending time with? Who might they be?

➤ If we ridicule, judge, or fight against someone, who are we really doing that to?

STEP THREE:

CHARACTER

It's nice to be thought of, and it's great when a friend calls you to say, "Hey, how are you doing, are you okay?"

But it's the friend who calls to say, "Listen, we're cooking dinner, come on over. I don't care if you've got a bad cold; I'm going to love you anyway."

Think about what that does.

It's not the people who call you. It's the ones who'd go to war for you, saying to others, hey, this is my friend. That's totally different. Being that sort of friend requires a person going above and beyond, offering a type of kindness and consideration that almost seems to defy logic, making recipients ask the question, "Why are you doing this for me?" or, "What did I ever do to deserve this?"

There are people out there like that. One of them is Coach Mike Garland.

To form an image of what life was like for me as a kid growing up in our West Willow neighborhood in Michigan, it's important to note that roughly eighty percent of my friends and peers in that area were all raised by single moms. The deficit of fathers and men, especially men with character and leadership abilities, was huge. For us, there was, understandably, a lot of confusion on what it meant to be a man.

Mike Garland was the basketball coach at Belleville High School in Detroit. Being a visionary, he decided to start building his next generation of basketball players by training them before they got to his school. He reached into middle and even elementary schools in order to do this. When I was twelve, Coach Garland was picking up boys from all over our neighborhood in his beat up old red station wagon and taking them to the gym for practice.

Those that wanted in on Coach Garland's program had to be ready and waiting at six a.m. at one of the five West Willow pick up locations. Coach told us, "All right, you don't have to come, but these are the times and days I'm going to be there, and if you're not there, you're getting left behind."

That alone took us a long way, character wise. When you're twelve and have to be on time for something that's happening so early in the morning with a change of clothes, your lunch, and everything you'll need for school, you're learning so much about responsibility, accountability, and discipline. You're also learning to respect other people's

45

time, and to have integrity, and that's empowering.

Whenever my friends and I saw that old, beat-down red station wagon approaching, we'd laugh and start singing the theme song to the old TV show, "Sanford and Son", because it looked just like the car on that show. So we'd be standing there on the corner going, "Dunt-dunt-dunt-duh -duh, dunt-dunt-dunt-duh-duh-duh-duh-duh…"

Once we were inside the red station wagon, there was an unspoken rule that whenever Coach Garland was talking, we needed to close our mouths and listen. Here was this man who we knew was more than likely dead broke, driving that old broken down car, yet in a way that went beyond the physical, we somehow knew we were among greatness. There was a feeling that surrounded the man.

He drove us to school, and he drove us home, which added up to a lot of man hours of mentoring outside of any formal setting. We didn't know it then, but that red station wagon was a vehicle for building our character. Everyone that got into that car was carefully mentored for their upcoming transition into manhood. The conversations we had were not exclusive to basketball; we talked about our families, about what we ate, our relationships with girls. We talked about our lives and visions for the future. To us, the red station wagon symbolized all of that. It affected everyone who got into it.

Mike Garland emerged in my life and presented a clear picture of what it looked like to be a man. The word that stands out to describe him, more than any other word, is integrity. He taught me to define who I was, what my mission was going to be, what I stood for, what I believed in. And then he taught me to stick all of that into the ground in an immovable way, no matter the circumstance, financial situation, or status. He showed us how to stand firm and say, "This is who I am."

As Coach Garland became more and more well-known, colleges from all over the country began trying to recruit him. A brilliant career and a much better salary awaited; yet he told me he would stay at Belleville until I graduated. He wanted to make sure I was going to get out of the West Willow situation, wanted to make sure I was going to be okay.

I can't help but ask myself, who would do that?

It stuns me to think that had Mike Garland just been doing his straight job, he'd never have known me. He wasn't getting paid to pick up twelve-year-olds at six a.m., no one made him do that. But his extra effort profoundly changed the course of my life.

When I signed my letter of intent to play college basketball at Idaho State University, Coach Garland signed a contract with Michigan State University. If you have followed Michigan State's history, you'd know that for the past decade, they've had one of the premiere basketball programs in the country. As a part of Coach Tom Izzo's basketball staff, Mike Garland continues to influence countless young men.

Coach Garland was unsure of what any of us would become, yet he invested, built up, and gave to us, anyway. Playing a major role, providing a blueprint for becoming a man. There I was at age twelve, trying to figure out how to do that from the examples of my peers and the older men on the block. The problem was, they didn't have any idea, since they didn't have fathers, either. I was studying the notes of flawed test-takers until along came Coach Garland, who was raising his family well, honoring his wife, and into community building.

His intent was to give us the information, speaking that kind of truth, so that instead of falling victim to the environment of the streets, each one of us had options. It was a game-changer.

Again, we didn't realize the value of what he was doing at the time, and I think that's typical. Being a mentor is a selfless position. Often those being mentored are far too self-absorbed, too wrapped up in their own problems to even think about extending gratitude. By the time the "students" figure it out, mentors have either passed on or are in positions where they're no longer accessible. The "thank you" doesn't come as often as it should.

When Coach Mike Garland was involved with an international basketball championship in 2000, none of us were surprised. Those who'd been given rides to and from school in that red station wagon always knew that was in him.

Because of Mike Garland's influence, I became a coach. While I coached a player named Randy Livingston, (the best point guard in Louisiana State University history), Randy kept saying, "I've got to introduce you to someone."

He introduced me to Coach Dale Brown.

Dale Brown recruited Shaquille O' Neal, brought him to America, signed him up at Louisiana State University, and coached him. "Shaq" later went on to become the best NBA center in basketball history. I first met Coach Brown at a famous restaurant in Baton Rouge, Louisiana, where "Shaq's" shoes were on display.

Could Coach Dale Brown have a big ego? Absolutely, and why not?

47

Look what he's done in his lifetime. It would be easy to get caught up in the status, the politics. But the amazing thing about Coach Brown is how he gives the same level of value to everyone. That's one of the reasons he and I clicked like we did, forming a friendship that's lasted for over thirty years. Coach Brown took me under his wing and had a tremendous impact on me, and he also helped me to understand the importance of character.

Coach Brown has had many good mentors, and one of them has been Coach John Wooden, the "father of basketball", the subject of multiple books, and of the Wooden Leadership Principles. There are those who say he's one of the best coaches that ever lived, and because of the mentoring, I'm just one person removed from him, through Coach Dale Brown.

So how is it that a man who grew up without a father could have had so many of the top male role models as mentors? That's just how powerful God is. He chose father figures for me from among the strongest, wisest, most loyal men in my country, and I'll be forever grateful.

I never played for Coach Dale Brown; I was introduced to him by a third party (Randy) who felt strongly that I needed to meet him. And had Coach Mike Garland been doing his job and only his job, he'd have only been working with high school students. Yet to this day, I could send either of them an email or call them on the phone and get a response. And that's not necessarily because I'm special. It's because they are.

Being That Friend and Discerning Your True Friends

If you have people in your life that would go to war for you, you know what that does. If you don't, you can become that person for someone else, and it will have the same positive effect.

Being there for people, what I call "coming along side of", builds character. You'll be filled up on a spiritual level, and feel you have a purpose. People will begin to tell you that you've made a difference. "Here's where I went after you came across the street to hug me," "Here's what I gave others after you gave to me."

You'll start feeling pretty good about who you are and why you're here.

I have a friend who's really been there for me lately, more so than in the past few years. When I thanked him for that and acknowledged all he'd done, he got emotional, I think because it dawned on him how he really hadn't been there, but now he is. He had regrets, but he remedied them. That's something to be proud of.

I have a lot of Caucasian acquaintances that claim to be my friends, but the truth is, they've never really come alongside me. They like their safe space in our friendship. Those who choose to come alongside me are those willing to say, "Derrick is my guy". The more friends I have that are willing to stand beside me in public, (without worrying about "getting dirty", or how they're going to "smell"), the more we'll eradicate divisive misperceptions.

A have a friend that's a high level executive, makes a lot of money, and drives a fancy car. We used to talk about everything together, we did all the stuff that friends do, but he's never come alongside me. These days as I'm traveling the world and growing my influence, he's suddenly interested in being there, but several years ago when I really needed him to come alongside me, he couldn't. He got the kind of exchange that we're having now, but it was all done in private, and no one knew that he was my friend.

My point is about character. If any kind of relationship is not loving, open, and public, then that person is not really your friend.

That said, we have no power to change anyone else, we can only change ourselves, so let's start there.

Do Something

Here's a fact: You cannot become who you want to be by remaining where you are.

You can accept things as they are, but that won't mean you'll stay where you are. The reality is that you're going to regress, backslide. So, you have two choices. You can decide you're all right with what is, and do nothing, knowing you'll not only not grow, but that your character will shrink. Or, you can take on the responsibility of changing things up, knowing that doing nothing is the saddest choice you can make.

It's never too late to choose to grow. Martin Luther King said, "The time is always right to do the right thing," and that includes doing the right thing for you.

Isn't it time for that?

If you believe in a higher power, you'll know you won't be going through this growth alone.

How You're Viewed by Others

If you're looking around, comparing where you are to those around you, you should stop. Everyone's walking their own path. The only person you should try to be better than is the "you" of yesterday.

Although you shouldn't be taking in a lot of what other people might say about you, there are times when that feedback might be helpful. I would say that the old adage, "where there's smoke, there's fire" might be true about seventy-five percent of the time. If someone says something about you that might be hurtful, before you toss that out, consider it for just a moment. If someone calls you selfish, and then a week later you hear the exact same thing from a completely different person that doesn't even know the first person who said that to you, that's something you need to take a look at closely. If a certain description doesn't go away and keeps coming back, those are clues you can utilize for discernment when it comes to who you are right now.

Surround Yourself with Good People

If you truly want to build your character, one of the surest ways to do that is to surround yourself with people you look up to and whose qualities you'd want to take on.

It's very true that "like attracts like". Without your saying one word, anyone can tell what kind of a person you are by the company you keep. Your friends say a lot about you, so make and keep good friends.

Because I've begun to understand that concept, I decided that I was only going to surround myself with people who were building something. If you see someone around me, you can know for sure that they're builders.

Those placed in your life are there for a reason, even if it's just to learn lessons from them. The idea is to constantly be moving forward. And here's the whole truth about people in your life: most are meant to pass through, and here's why. Because if you're constantly learning, growing, and expanding, a lot of the people you'll meet are only going to be in your life for a season, until you learn what you're supposed to learn from them, and then it's time to move on. There's only so far you can go with someone who is learning from you, and you from them, until the growth stops. You grow, or they grow, and one of you grows to the point that it exceeds the relationship. When that happens, it's time to move on. That doesn't mean you don't care about that person, or that you're no longer friends. There's just a shift in where you're supposed to spend your time.

The key is finding those people who care about you and challenge you to constantly improve, be better, because as you know, when it comes to how you spend your time, you're either growing or you're not.

Iron Sharpens Iron

It's scientific knowledge that iron sharpens iron. That also applies to people. Those who are sharp and on the ball hang out with others of equal skill to make both better people.

A friend of mine, Dr. Ivan Misner, likes to say, "If you were in a room where there was only one way in, and no way out, who would you let into that room?"

We all know people who are in drama, or who are negative. There are those who are always going to be tearing you down, or who only pretend to be your friend. Would you let them in? Because in this scenario, they can never get back out. By the same token, you really have to be careful about who you allow to come into your circle.

Here's the catch. In order for the "iron sharpens iron" to work, both individuals have to be iron, so think deeply about who you're letting in.

You Become Like Those You Spend Your Time With

Our society might think that it's okay to have friends who are doing drugs and doing a lot of drinking. Our society might think that to be a true friend, you need to keep hanging out with that person, and help them.

Let me just say this: You might not be doing drugs or drinking, or be committing some of the crimes those around you are committing, but if you think you're going to stay out of that, allow me to give you a reality check. You're already in it. You are already in it. It's only a matter of time before you're influenced. You might not engage in the conduct, but you're already regarded as someone who spends time with those who do drugs, and that negatively impacts your potential for job opportunities, how adults and other community leaders view you, your trust factor decreases, and the list goes on and on.

Bad associations spoil useful elements. The need to be careful about who we align ourselves with exists. From our political leadership to the kids on the playground, all the way down the line.

Solitude

While it is an excellent thing to surround yourself with those who will influence you positively, it's also highly recommended that you listen to your own inner voice. If you're always around a lot of people, you won't be able to connect with yourself.

I spent a lot of time alone when I was younger, and I still take time to be alone these days, because there is such power in solitude. There are so many things you can learn from being in silence, taking time to acknowledge your thoughts. There is a strength and energy that comes from solitude that shouldn't be overlooked on your journey towards becoming what you want to be.

Take some time each day to shut out the voices, the noise, the activity rushing all around, and check in with yourself.

Respect Yourself and Others Will Respect You

Once you have good people around who are positively influencing you, and once you've gotten into the habit of spending time on your own in order to appreciate who and what you are, you'll be less willing to let others push you around. You've now become your own best investment, and you've put some time and effort into improving yourself.

If you honestly respect yourself, that's going to be obvious to those around you, and they will follow your lead. You will be the one who sets the example for how to treat you. When you treat yourself with respect, others will follow. You lead out.

Be Authentic

One very old saying is the admonition not to "hide your light under a bushel". In my mind, this goes right along with "are you who you say you are"?

If you're downplaying who you are, that's falsehood. If you have a talent that you never speak up about, a strength you keep hidden, or a spiritual way of living or belief system that's placed out of the public eye, you are not who you say you are.

Another thing we're taught from our society is to have this false humility. We're told not to "toot our own horn" and not to talk much about our accomplishments. I feel some conflict with that, I get it. We all want to receive accolades and we all want to be lifted up in the public eye, but much of our society tells us not to do that.

Due to this, our generation is downplaying their gifts. The student on the back row in class won't tell you that he's been playing the guitar for the past seven years, that he's one of the best guitar players in the state, has traveled to national conferences to play at events. The girl who seems so shallow around her girlfriends isn't going to divulge that she's painted the most incredible works of art, which she keeps in her room at home. Our kids are hiding their light, and we're hiding our light.

Why is it that we're all so afraid to declare, "I am who I say I am"?

If that's who you are, that's who you are! But, think about it, now. How do the masses benefit if they say they don't want you to "toot your own horn"? Why would that be a popular thing to preach?

I'll tell you. If you're not fantastic, I don't have to be fantastic, and if I don't have to be fantastic, I don't have to put forth any effort. I don't have to shine, I don't have to lead, and I don't have to use any courage at all.

I used to hear it said all the time that we're "losing our edge". From a systematic perspective, this false humility we've encouraged has created a wave of mediocrity. It's not who we are, so that's a lie. And if "iron sharpens iron", certainly "dullness encourages dullness".

If you're a six foot five black man with an MBA, make sure people know about it. If during the weekdays you're a college professor, do not play that down, either. If you sing, if you write, if you're an artist, if you passionately believe in a cause or adhere to a religion that you're fervent about, it's okay to share.

Shatter Stereotypes

It is our responsibility to shatter stereotypes.

Society had a pessimistic view of people like me, coming from Detroit. There were some bleak statistics stacked up against me, indicating that children like me would never amount to anything. I decided to overcome those adversities and stepped outside of the box, and I'm not about to pretend my past never happened. We've got to show people who we really are, show them our truth, because it's not their job to excavate it. That's on us.

Stand Up, Speak Out, and Own What You Say

I've organized the L.E.A.D.E.R.S.H.I.P. Ambassador program. When youth attend L.E.A.D.E.R.S.H.I.P. meetings, any time a youth there wants to say something, they have to physically stand up. And then everyone else has to shut up. This teaches the undercurrent of connectivity in everything we do.

If someone has something they feel they need to say, a thought that's inspired, everyone in that room needs to be silent. Then the one holding the stage has the opportunity to stand up and own what it is they're preparing to say, because as soon as it leaves their lips, it's going to be theirs, they'll be accountable for those words.

Today's technology doesn't teach this, it allows us to dissociate the words coming from us, with very little accountability. There are even those who create mock profiles on social media in order to send out words that hold darkness without fear of repercussion, or something that can't be taken back is sent out over the phone. They never think it will come back to them. As technology advances, that is only going to get worse.

When a person states their thoughts while standing and in person, that teaches them the gravity of their words, and also teaches them to choose those words carefully. There is no substitute for face-to-face, responsible interaction.

In order to avoid social breakdown, we need to continue to educate our youth, and to help them understand and respect themselves and each other. As a community, we can become an extension of their influential leadership, as well as set an example for our children. We can teach them that real integrity is doing the right thing, on or offline.

Have a Vehicle

I'm going to pass on the same message that Coach Garland and Coach Brown have: you are valued, and because you have value, you can be more. Their wisdom and energy have created a legacy.

Not too long ago, I put together some YouTube videos called "365 Days of Inspiration". It was just something I started doing, thinking it would be a good idea. Each segment was filmed from the viewpoint of a passenger seat, as I'm driving to a school. I thought that would be a good way to approach people, especially youth, not even connecting the dots that I was emanating what had been done for me in those early years, recreating that very same dynamic. When I did make the connection, it got me thinking.

Coach Garland literally had a vehicle for teaching, for carrying people to the places they needed to go. If you're going to lead, you're going to require a "vehicle" of some sort. It might be sports, or dancing, or art, music. It doesn't matter what it is, you just need to have something that your followers can "get into".

Speak Life

My personal gift might not be wowing people with intellect, and that's okay. The gift I've been given to convey is that of truth. When I talk to the youth, that's what I use, truth, and I'm just real with them. I do the same thing with adults, and have learned to be that person who is willing to identify the "elephant" in the room that no one wants to talk about. Anyone who lives and speaks out in truth will eventually find themselves looking forward to opportunities to do this, because those willing to step up and start leading will be those who come to know they're making a difference in this world, and that's ultimately satisfying.

I've done a few in-service meetings at schools, addressing their leadership population. When I'm aware there are student behavior problems and bullying within a particular school's walls, I say to those leaders, in essence, "What you're seeing is a byproduct of your leadership."

(I need to add here that the reason I can speak such truth is that no one owns me. I haven't signed on with any big sponsors, I'm not on that school district's payroll, and my boss is not in the room giving me the eye. I'm my own boss, so that gives me a lot of freedom to say what needs to be said.)

There is often a pause and some silence as those at the in-service take the "this is a byproduct of your leadership" statement in, and you can almost read their thoughts through their expressions as the people in the room either deny or acknowledge. If acknowledged, there are times when administrators will open the discussion further, and apologize for actions they've realized as erroneous and harmful. They might even get emotional as barriers break down, and this allows additional light to be shed on the meeting as others follow suit, come to realizations, and begin to change.

This is what happens when you apply truth. It pierces people's spirits to the point that they say, "Okay." Then we peel back all of the fancy degrees, the titles, the nice cars, and every other façade, and get down to who they really are. This is the benefit of speaking truth. Speaking truth is speaking life, and something happens during the process: everyone within earshot of truth is changed. When someone speaks truth, it not only helps others, it helps the person speaking it, too.

You can tell if you're speaking truth if it is accompanied by forward motion. Falsehood creates the opposite. People close up, retreat, and things come to a halt. Lies and falsehood are death. Truth is life.

That's likely one of the reasons why Martin Luther King, Jr. said that when you don't stand up for right, truth, and justice, you die.

We don't want to die, we want to live.

Everyone Can Speak Truth, but Not Everyone Will

There have been both youth and adults that look around and see what I've been involved in, and want to get involved. Some are extremely helpful to the cause, assisting with the momentum and growth. Others say they want to become involved with Stand Up, but it's clear that although they might want to vicariously live, be, do, speak, and operate in the spaces Stand Up is operating in, they're not willing to risk or sacrifice anything. They can't let go or step out, they're not comfortable with being that light; they feel it's just too risky, so instead they're just fans.

We have a "fifteen minutes of fame" society that's loaded with real-time gratification, and people are forgetting that true greatness is a process. It doesn't come from creating a clever marketing concept, a catchy tagline, or a strong statement. Greatness is a process, one that disallows a person to remain in mediocrity and luke-warmth. As each day goes by, we're either getting better or we're getting worse, and we know which is which.

When it comes to truth, start with yourself. Do you like where you are right now, and do you like where you're headed?

Absolutely everyone can improve, and the best day to make some changes is today.

Leadership

Ancient prophesies warn of wide spread drought, and we're entering into that space now when it comes to a lack of leadership. Our world is in desperate need for people to stand up, from parents to educators, policepersons to business owners, there's a long list. The good news is, there is a need, meaning there are open slots for so many who desire to lead well.

Adult leaders have such tremendous potential when it comes to influencing our youth, and our youth will then be leaders who are accountable for altering the world's future for the better. They're hungry for solid teaching and mentoring, and they're willing to emulate the behavior of those around them. If you don't believe me, just think of the structure of a gang. As our children grow, their minds also grow and expand, and those minds are yearning to be filled with knowledge.

What are we going to pour into those minds?

I can tell you that I'm where I'm at today, largely due to those who've taken the time to heavily influence my life. My mother laid the foundation for what I am, and then that was taken to the next level by my basketball coach and personal mentor, Mike Garland.

When considering that man's unlikely background, his family structure, educational history, and limited resources, what will forever stand out is his ultimate selflessness.

We both came from families who had nothing, so we related to each other and that institutionalized poverty. Yet Coach Mike gave me inspirational and motivational wealth, in an invaluable blueprint for manhood, and that's what allowed me to break out of educational and intellectual poverty. He left his circumstances and is now a six-figure man, one of the top coaches in the U.S. He got himself a different kind of life, and then showed me how to do the same.

We have an obligation to strive for excellence, because we cannot lead unless we go first. Then, we have an obligation to pass on that motivation to strive, and to give youth the tools to make wise, life enhancing decisions. If we're being our authentic, truthful selves, this won't take a lot of preaching. There will be those who see what we have, and want to follow, and it's our job to invite them on that journey.

As with Coach Mike Garland, who was so selfless with his time and intellectual resources, we can help others by letting go of our selfishness, and by making ourselves available as mentors.

You Don't Have to Know it All

I'm sure you've heard that "with leadership comes responsibility". Part of that responsibility lies in not trying to have all of the answers all of the time. No one is all knowing, and it's falsehood to pretend to be. There are times that we have to admit that we just don't know, or don't currently have the solution. That's the time when instead of a lot of talk, we need to just be quiet and listen.

I continue to understand that the best answers are the ones that arrive when you take some time in solitude and call on your spirit.

People have said to me, "Wow, you're a natural leader", and that's nice. I've been given some gifts, for which I'm grateful. The gift of size (no one is going to overlook me), and the ability to communicate ideas effectively. That's the external stuff.

But it's the internal stuff that's powerful, and that doesn't come cheap.

When others say, "Where did you come from?" (in essence, wanting to know how I showed up from what looked like out of the blue, to create a fast-growing, much needed movement). I've been right here all along, but like those plants that go underground for a while to prepare for the outward growing season, I've been being developed underground, having my useful winter. All of us will need to take that kind of time. We'll need to be still, get our answers, and work on this person we're becoming. Remember, it's a process.

Opposition is Just Part of the Workout

Know that if you're going to live in the stream of your purpose, it's not going to be easy. Accept that right now as a part of the gift of walking your path; that the opposition you'll face at times might seem insurmountable. There will always be forces fighting against something that is happening for the greater good, so if you have opposition, rest assured that you're most likely on the right path.

I can tell you this: After a while, you get used to that workout, and once you're used to it you'll have gained some strong leadership muscles, strong enough that no one is going to be able to sway you or push you around. You will have developed a confidence and the ability to live daily with no small degree of vision.

Having said that, I want to state again how imperative it is that you understand what your purpose is, that you have a clear view of what you want your future to look like, so that you can lead by example without faltering.

My future was supposedly predestined. Coach Mike Garland and others set me on the path to something different, and then those leaders of mine stayed steady for me. That's something else to consider when you're gearing up to be a leader. Once you're leading, you have to be vigilant. Understand and pay attention to your blind spots with some good old fashioned common sense, and be realistic about your weaknesses so they won't become your downfall.

When you're a leader, it's not just about you anymore. For the sake of those you're leading, once you begin, you need to keep going, because slipping up and doing something selfish will hurt those who've chosen to follow your lead and your example. There have been some very famous people within the black community that have been held in high regard, they've changed the face of things, helped to reframe how the black family structure should look. Opened people's minds to new possibilities. But when those leaders fall, it's destructive.

You've absolutely, absolutely got to endure to the end.

This is why some shy away from leadership. If no one's following you, it's just you. If you make a mistake in judgment, you only have to be sorry to you. The more followers you have, the more people are listening to what you say and observing what you do, changing their mindsets from what they've heard and seen. The ripple effect of a scandal can be devastating, undo the good that's been done, and cause harm that continues for years.

Lessons/ Trials

Everyone goes through trials, but how they're endured depends upon how they're viewed. It's beneficial to understand that there's a pattern to our trials. If we don't absorb the lesson of one trial, that trial will reemerge in another form until we "get it", and truthfully address the message. (Not unlike the man on the street in Sydney).

Like it or not, this process will continue throughout your entire life. Nothing grows without some stretching and a little pain, and we humans are creatures of growth. While it's true that we can mature physically without growing mentally and emotionally, "growing up" does not solve the problems or help you to avoid your lessons. Growing up doesn't make things better.

True growth is cumulative, occurring one day at a time, one lesson at a time, unless you refuse to learn the lessons placed before you, and then your growth can be thwarted.

So understand that the lessons are placed on your daily path for your benefit by a higher power, be thankful for that, and joyfully grow, knowing each lesson is a step towards what you are supposed to become.

You Are the Hero You're Looking For

It's hard not to get down when looking around at the hypocrisy within our society today. There's too much talking, too much politics, and too many excuses.

Too many are standing on the sidelines, when the truth is that every one of us is needed. We all need to get in the game. All of us need to stand up and become a part of the solution.

We can make all the excuses we want, but that doesn't change the fact that despite the excuses and explanations, we're needed.

People say this world needs another Martin Luther King, another Mother Theresa. Did you ever stop to think that YOU are the hero you're looking for?

So what are you going to stand up for? What will you no longer tolerate? I'm not necessarily asking you to come and join Stand Up, I'm just asking you to stand up, period. Stand up for those things that only you could know; those things that are very personal to you that are happening within your circle.

You stand up and decide to serve and lead those within your circle of influence, and there's no limit to the growth your character can experience, or to the miracles that can happen.

Let's Talk

➢ What is one very good way to build character?

➢ How can others quickly tell what you're like without really knowing you?

➢ If you're constantly learning and growing, what will happen with your relationships?

➢ Who would you allow into your room where there's only one way in and no way out?

➢ Why is it important to choose your company wisely?

➢ What role does solitude play in building your character? What times can you carve out in your daily schedule to get that solitude?

➢ What might stop you from adhering fully to the phrase, "I am who I say I am"?

➢ How might you "shatter" peoples' stereotypes of you?

➢ What are some physical ways to become more accountable for your words?

➢ How can you tell if you're speaking truth?

> ➤ How can you fill the leadership void? Where can you see a lack of quality leadership, and how might you help?

> ➤ What should you do if you don't know the answers at first?

> ➤ What do you need to get used to before you can build some strong leadership muscles?

> ➤ What can happen to a person's leadership if a leader is involved in a scandal? Have you ever seen this happen? What were the ripples from that?

> ➤ Who is the hero you're looking for?

STEP FOUR:

CRITICAL THINKING

Clear, reasoned thinking and the ability to make well thought out judgments is invaluable.

Everything starts with an idea in your mind, a goal. In order to reach that goal, envision the sight of yourself diligently striving, and then meeting that goal. Use your imagination and add in as many details as you can, make what you're seeing as realistic as possible, and employ the power of positive thinking.

Play it out in your mind like this: "If I take this action, then this will happen, and if I take this other action, then this will happen." Having the ability to predict the result of those actions is called critical thinking.

The more you walk within your purpose, the more clarity and common sense you'll have that will assist you in your critical thinking, and you'll often find yourself saying, "Oh, if I go over there, that's going to take me off purpose. That's not even in my stream, so you know what? I'm not going to do that."

Some horrifying things happened not long ago that affected me and the rest of our country, and I was in sorrow about them. Because of the role I'm in with Stand Up, people wanted me to make a public statement about the recent events. There was a lot of gloom and negativity surrounding that time, and I wanted to weigh in with a fresh perspective, but also, if possible, a positive, hopeful perspective.

I'd been in prayer and had managed to keep quiet for days, wanting to make sure the response I gave came from wisdom and not just pure emotion.

When emotion dictates our decisions about the words we say and actions we take, it might feel "right" at the moment, but that doesn't mean it is right. Emotions can make it hard to separate and discern feelings from reality. Just because something's pulling at you emotionally doesn't mean it's the correct choice. We've seen plenty of people make harmful decisions or even die from the "heat of the moment".

If your decisions are not in alignment with what you're called to do, or if by using your powers of critical thinking, you can see that a choice is going to cause you to back slide, you know you can't make that choice. You can't go back to being that person, because it's not where your purpose is. You just have to honor that and move forward.

Consider that if you are led by your emotions and take a few steps backwards, you're not leading or helping anybody, and you could possibly hurt a lot of people.

When I rode the ElliptiGo across America, I had only two rules. Rule Number One was that my driver and I would not pick anything up. I didn't care if there was a bag of money sitting on the side of the road with a hundred thousand dollars inside, we wouldn't touch it.

Rule Number Two was that we would never go backwards. If I happened to lose my cell phone in Mesa, Arizona, I wouldn't go back.

Not going back proved to be a very good idea, and that rule alone might very well have saved our lives more than a few times. I don't like to talk about it a lot, but some of the areas I rode through were so dangerous, do deadly. I knew that if I went back through them a second time, I wouldn't have made it out of those places alive. Someone who meant me harm would have been ready and waiting.

There were places where the racism and hatred was almost tangible as I pedaled past Confederate flags and other symbols of separatism. Believe me, it was the real deal, and here I was, often alone, riding on a stand up elliptical thinking, wow, I've got to keep moving ahead, I've just got to stay focused.

That same sort of thinking is so true to life. If you backpedal to a place in your life where you used to be, the opposition that knows your past might be your weakness is lying in wait for you. But many times people think they can go back and remain unscathed. That's a lie. You cannot go back. The opposition is right there, waiting to say, "we gotcha".

Once you go back, things will be worse than before, and not only will you not be able to help anyone else, it will be much harder to help yourself.

Widespread Lack of Critical Thinking

In many places, especially where I come from, the encouragement of critical thinking practices is practically nonexistent, and thinking from pure emotion is rampant. Very few are talking about critical thinking, character, courage, and common sense.

Watching tragedy happening on both sides of the fence is a reflection of the absence of the teaching of these things.

Where is the common sense in grabbing for your gun when in the presence of the local authorities? Critical thinking puts those thoughts into place that will help you to survive, which is the main goal at a tense time like that. Whatever you do is with the aim to survive. It stands to reason that if you'll agree to lie down as asked and put your arms out, you'll probably live. If you stay upright and lift your shirt to reveal what looks like a semi-automatic handgun, then the chances that you might die are higher.

This doesn't excuse the other side's critical thinking. If there is a true need to shoot in self-defense, it can be to maim, not to kill. Removing the emotion and employing critical thinking turns would-be headlines into instances where people can continue to live and move beyond the incident.

The need for critical thinking in everyone is imperative.

Think Ahead

When choices are being made, not enough people are asking themselves the question, "To what end?" In other words, "If I do this, what will be the end result?"

Outcomes aren't being weighed out nearly enough, there isn't enough time being taken to gauge an event and reach the best decision. There needs to be enough delay for a person to stop, think, and ask themselves, "Okay, how am I going to respond?"

I've had some experience with this as a youth, having been in situations with law enforcement that could easily have gone tragically wrong. Because I'd learned about and had been practicing critical thinking, I made sure things did not go wrong.

Something I have no delusions about is my appearance. A six foot five, three hundred pound black man is not an inviting scenario to an officer of the law that might be thinking about making an arrest. They're not especially looking forward to that experience. I had to be willing to make any exchanges as easy, non-confrontational, and uneventful as humanly possible. That required critical thinking.

When You're Not Sure

We've talked before about not having all the answers all of the time, and there will be instances where it might look like you're required to give a response or come up with an answer right away. Again, when you don't know, be still, and if you need to come right out and say, "I don't know, so I'm not going to do anything with it at the moment," then say it. That's powerful. If you're still and not acting out in emotion, you'll have nothing to clean up afterwards.

If more people would be still for a time, more would come back to situations with clear and concise voices that would speak volumes in times of tension. That sort of thing, if repeated enough times by enough voices, could change the world.

But if people don't take delay to listen, they respond out of chaos, and create more chaos, and there is no message but anger within that kind of response.

I'm certainly not a perfect person. I struggle just like everyone else with anger, sorrow, and disappointment; when those things are present, there is a fog around my personal mission. When this happens, I employ solitude and don't hang out with anyone when I'm going through the process of being in prayer and getting my vision and clarity back. This works, in order to return to a place of peace where I just love people.

An Honest Assessment

We talked about my being aware of my physical appearance, and that's a part of critical thinking. How you look is something to have a good reality of. It's not anyone else's responsibility but our own to be aware of that. We need to understand how we are perceived, because that's a part of what will determine the final outcome in any given situation.

There are plenty of people who get angry for being treated like they're punks, but if you're wearing a pair of baggy pants and a hoodie, you're contributing to getting treated like a punk. It's not God's way, but humans do judge by what they see. When you're wearing saggy jeans that show your underwear, for much of the population of the world, that says "punk".

Within entire communities, this expression through wardrobe is being used as a method of rebellion against social norms, and within entire communities there are a disproportionate number of arrests, incarcerations, and disenfranchisement.

The message that the wardrobe and behavior sends is, "Instead of conforming to how I think you want me to be, I'm going to do the total opposite, because I think you hate me, and I think I hate you, too."

There are entire communities where anarchy is simmering, especially among those that feel they are being treated like they're of the second class, but they're not understanding their contribution to the problem.

I talked to a friend of mine just a couple of weeks ago, saying, "Okay, you're a good guy, but nobody's hiring you, and you need to be working. You've got a family that needs to eat, but you're not getting hired, because you are being viewed as a threat to society. Because of your appearance, you're not being given job opportunities, and the government isn't helping you out anymore, either. The government thinks you've taken advantage of the system they've provided. If you want to get a job, here's the reality..."

I spoke truth to him, so he'd take a look at what those who were on the outside looking in saw. How does it feel, I wonder, to be that man and not recognize that?

People aren't willing to speak truth, and sometimes even when it's spoken, they're not willing to hear it. What they are willing to do is continue to operate under that kind of liability, instead of gaining some legitimacy and some employable qualifications. If a person doesn't have the skill set that's being sought when it comes to employment, they need to both get the skill set, and look the part. But, it's much easier to keep the attitude instead of having that frank conversation with each other and provide a teaching moment. What's being created in its place is hostility and an even more divisive relationship between the "have's" and "have not's".

It's far easier to brush off putting forth some effort and say of the negative experience, "It's because I'm black, or overweight, or because of my gender, or because I'm not beautiful", but that's a cop out. Let's use some common sense and critical thinking again: It's not because you're black. It's because you're wearing your pants down around your knees, and you look just like you're getting ready to go rob a convenience store.

In a perfect world, a person should not be judged for their looks, but the bottom line most of the time boils down to our behavior. Even if a person's wearing baggy jeans and they're not willing to change that, they can still behave well, do the "unexpected". Behavior is usually what determines the final outcome and good behavior is a part of shattering stereotypes.

Shatter that stereotype. Think for yourself. Be different than the rest who aren't using their critical thinking power, those who are listening to that same old tired record that are too unambitious to question if that's really how things are.

Standing Up and Standing Out

I'm from the "'hood", a place where most guys don't get out. I know very well that when you start doing things at a higher level, there's a fair amount of guilt that's going to get heaped onto you from the others. They'll try their best to make you feel bad, and, (here's that emotional part again), the cut of "you must think you're better than us, you must think you're big time now".

Know this: the mockery isn't really about you. You're stepping out and growing out of that mediocre role, and it's making those around you feel insecure. It's causing them to reexamine their lives, and either be compelled to expand or fight to stay the same. If they don't want to expand, they're going to try to stop you from doing their thing, so that they're once again comfortable. The mockery is all about them, not about you.

Remember the rule. You love them, but you can't go back. A good example of why comes from several black professional athletes who've experienced a tremendous downfall. To figure out the reason why, all you have to do is take a look at who they chose to be around. 80-90% of them went back to their old neighborhoods and tried to bring their boys back with them. They both went back and picked something up.

When cycling across American, my driver and I had a situation where those rules weren't followed, and it almost got Andrew, my driver, killed. In Port Angeles, Washington, while on the ElliptiGo, I met another guy who was riding his bike around the circumference of America, and our paths happened to intersect. The man had been sleeping on the side of the freeway, randomly ate off and on, had no money, was pretty much homeless, and was strung out on drugs. I felt in my spirit that I needed to stay away from this person. So I cycled away from him and continued on my ride. My driver was twenty miles behind me and didn't know of my decision not to ride near the other cyclist. He had no idea I'd already talked to this man.

Something else my driver had done previously was to pick up a lock knife switchblade he found on the side of the road. One rule, already busted.

So I'm twenty miles ahead, and my driver did as he always had, drove a little, then waited about two hours until I was another twenty miles down the road, and then he drove again. So, he's waiting, and the other cyclist rides up next to the RV, enters the RV, and the first thing he grabs off the counter is that lock knife.

So a strange man's in the RV with my driver, and now he's got a knife. The deranged man, holding the knife, demanded that Andrew give him some food. Andrew had just been microwaving two frozen croissants, and handed them over. The cyclist stood there eating them, all the while holding that knife as Andrew sat there, watching him and scared to death.

While the man was still wolfing down the croissants, someone else banged on the door of the RV.

It was a state trooper who had pulled over because there was an RV parked along the freeway, and in that state that wasn't allowed.

Both men were asked to exit the RV, and the trooper quickly assessed the situation. The cyclist was obviously under the influence of something, and the trooper felt there was a good chance that had he not interrupted, the man might have killed Andrew. He allowed Andrew to drive away in the RV while he stayed behind with that cyclist.

Understand that by picking something up, everything was prime for things to go south. When I later asked Andrew why he picked up the knife in the first place, he gave an answer that many of us have used before. He simply said, "I don't know."

Lesson: don't pick anything up. Not old habits, friends that don't serve you, and no matter what, don't turn back.

If you go back to where you came from and try to save them all, you're picking something up that's going to slow down your journey, and then you won't be able to help anyone at all. The best you can do for yourself and anybody else that you might lead in the future is to move forward and pave the way for them to follow. If you do that, there might come a day when they can walk towards you.

Think About It

Let's go back to what Andrew said when I asked him why he'd picked up that knife:

"I don't know."

If you don't know why you're doing something, then don't do it. Simple as that. One of the models I used on a constant basis is to observe, assess, and then reach a hypothesis before making any final decisions. Most people aren't aware of just how fragile their lives are, or how quickly a scenario can change from decisions made. In order to survive and thrive, critical thinking is required on a daily basis. There will always be events that will occur. Fires, over-drawn bank accounts, an argument or end of a relationship, cars running out of gas. That stuff's always going to happen. What we're missing is the ability to process multiple outcomes, based upon the ways we respond.

Are you aware that the way you choose to think in the morning and throughout your twenty-four hours on a daily basis vastly impacts what will happen throughout the rest of the day? As simple as that sounds, people still don't think through how their decisions can lead to either favorable or unfavorable outcomes. We truly have so much more power than we give ourselves credit for, but we're not observing, assessing, and creating these hypotheses in order to make educated, clear decisions. When we skip those three steps and make our choices, it's often to our detriment.

When I was attending college, I really struggled academically during the first three years. I was a solid student athlete, but the importance of the "student" part hadn't yet resonated with me.

It resonated, big time, when trying to maintain a 2.0 grade point average to stay eligible to play basketball. Each year, I needed to take and pass twenty four credits worth of classes, but I'd made the mistake of flunking a couple of classes, leaving me short two credits.

I remember sitting in the academic advisor's office, listening to her tell me that I was going to lose my scholarship, that I would no longer be a part of my basketball team.

When a person is in critical thinking mode, one of the first things to do is remove emotion. I can't stress this enough. You cannot get caught up in what's happening at the moment, and everything that goes with it that makes you so emotionally charged. You have to take a step away from all of that.

As a junior in college, I had to step back and think, okay, what are my options? What's really going to happen, here? I was able to narrow it all down to several things. My first intuition was that I should look beyond that academic advisor for the answers. I would not trust something as precious as my future to someone who told me at the end of the semester there were no classes available, there was nothing I could do to make up those credits.

Frustrated, I toyed with giving up and going back to Detroit, but knew that if I did, my life would have changed for the worse.

Knowing that no one was going to care about my life like I did, I decided to do my own research and found a three credit professional development class that was part of a continuing education unit. The class wasn't designed for my major, it was intended for social workers, but it could easily translate into the credits I needed for my academic purposes.

I attended the class eight hours a day for two or three weekends, and while I sat in that class I thought, man, what I'm learning is going to change the outcome of my life. What was taught there altered everything that had been getting ready to transpire, and all because of a decision not to just take someone's word for it, but to do my own due diligence and look for a solution.

That academic advisor worked fifty hour weeks, and hadn't looked into additional classes. The thought never occurred to her that a professional development class offered through a continuing education unit would transfer over.

Never allow your critical thinking to be outsourced. It's easy to do: we can be so busy and disengaged that we automatically default our decision-making to others in "authority", even with things that are directly connected to our future. Societies and governments perpetuate that, and that can often provide a false sense of security. In a cyclical way, we have become sheep. We don't question, we don't discern, and we don't look at the facts. Many of us just think, "Oh, well, that's the way it is."

If I had done that back then and returned to Detroit, I doubt I'd be doing what I'm doing today.

Critical thinking is observing, assessing, and coming up with a hypothesis. You go over the potential options, explore those options, and then you make a decision.

That's the model to use.

Your Critical Thinking Helps Others

Once you trust your instinct and intellect enough to guide you, you'll be much better equipped to help others recognize and reveal their hidden strengths. You can be the kind of leader that helps others to see what they can't yet see in themselves, and assist someone in their own critical thinking and decision making.

Don't make the mistake of believing that your day-to-day choices don't matter. I can tell you that there have been decisions made throughout my childhood that made a profound difference. Times where I didn't get into the car that later got shot up, or times when I didn't go to the party where someone was killed.

I think we all hold something inside that makes us question things more deeply, if we'll only acknowledge it. There have been times in my life that were tipping points leading to that next step. Why did I feel like I didn't want to live in Detroit, even though I'd grown up there? Why did I begin to question the things going on around me? Before I thought more into it, the questioning used to make me a little crazy, but there was something else at work, and I just had to find out what that was.

More recently, my ride across America was an extremely dangerous undertaking, and I had to listen to that intuition and employ critical thinking at every mile. Within the first two months after returning to Boise, where cycling is very popular, there were seven cycling fatalities involving automobiles. Seven. Part of my being kept safe was the use of critical thinking. I literally had to consider every choice, every turn, every conversation, and every person I was associating with, and I very much feel it was a trial run for the much bigger picture of my life.

If we get enough people who are learning to think this way, there will be a true and systematic shift within our lives, our homes, and our communities. An adult that masters critical thinking can influence the lives of youth who will one day be accountable for changing and improving the future. When you strengthen your thinking, it becomes so much bigger than you.

Looking Ahead

Part of an adult's critical thinking tools should include planting good seeds for a future harvest within the minds and hearts of our youth, the future leaders of tomorrow. Our children are hungry for knowledge, and much more intuitive and perceptive than they're given credit for. These kids are in the trenches, and to think they're not affected by the choices the adults in their lives make is short-sighted.

If we want to make a lasting impact on the future, we'll invest in the youth within our homes and our schools.

Make the Most of the Best

"Make the most of the best, and the least of the worst." Everything that surrounds us holds potential, but it's so easy and common to get caught up in the many activities that don't mean much. If a person intends to "make the most of the best", they improve and maximize everything and every situation presented. That's what great people do.

Conversely, if there's an unfortunate situation, you need to minimize that, shrink it down to its appropriate size in your mind, and then turn it into something that won't impact your direction in the future. "Make the most of the best, and the least of the worst."

Know Where You're Going

We must have purpose, something that is our motivation and holds deep meaning for us. If we're lacking that passion, if we don't have something that burns within our hearts, our days will be meaningless.

Each day when you wake up, you should be asking yourself, "What's driving me today? What is it that makes me want to get up and start this day?"

If you don't have an answer to that, lie there a little longer and find one.

We Can Create Our Own Culture

Who determines our culture? WE do. And we can create the kind of culture that speaks out against the things we see in the world that we don't like.

I recently put a post out on social media that summarized our current entertainment, and how we've let it become the teacher and mentor of our children. I said we needed to be careful about how we were allowing our modern entertainment to influence the next generation.

Where on TV and other entertainment sites are those who model for our young people the things they really need to know? They're not getting that from the "reality" shows, but those are the kinds of things our kids are consuming, and they're taking it in physically, emotionally, mentally, and spiritually.

They're filling their minds with story after story of cheaters and liars, thieves and murderers, and the all-too-true phrase "garbage in, garbage out" still applies. Then we wonder why we have kids with honesty, violence, and crime issues.

Because of our culture's entertainment, our children think this is the way the world is supposed to be, since they're not seeing anything else. Many parents are too busy to do the talking that would neutralize those beliefs, so those kids figure that this is just how it is, and they run with the general herd.

Again, it's the "elephant in the room".

We Own Our Happiness

One day I told a group of thirty five second graders some straight up truth.

I said that they all needed to go home and tell their parents, "If your life sucks, you're accountable for that."

I saw every one of those kids take in a breath.

I repeated, "Yeah. I want you to go tell your parents that I told you to say that."

This is serious: if the kids can stop and think, "Hey, wait a minute. All of this drama, this craziness, the girls or the boys don't like me, the social media messages...if all of that stuff sucks, I have directly or indirectly played a role toward the manifestation of that."

"Go tell your parents," I told them.

Don't Be Common

Rethink fitting in. Trying too hard to be accepted, a part of things, and being "in" is a large portion of the problem. Most of the commonalities in this world are things we should not be "common" about, we're actually just being thoughtless.

Critical thinking defines who you are, and allows you to have a direct impact on that process, versus letting others define who you are. You do not want to be indecisive about that, because one moment of indecision can turn you into the person who smokes marijuana and gets involved in car theft. Now you're really not able to create yourself, because you've just had a couple of extra labels tacked onto you for the rest of your life.

Going with the flow is never the right way to go.

When you become an individual, there's a domino effect that allows those around you to reconsider their choices, too.

Step by Step

Strong critical thinking and intuition don't happen all of a sudden.

A good example of this was the process involved with my ride across the U.S. At first, I had several celebrities pegged to do certain parts of the journey for the Stand Up cause, and it looked like that was going to work out until one by one, each fell away and had to cancel for different reasons. Little by little, the shape of the project changed, until the only person left to go was the one who came up with the idea: me.

Had I been inspired right away to take off and go cross country, my answer to that would have been "no". But the pace of those revelations was that of a slow drip that led up to the "aha" moment of how things were really supposed to be. In between, I took some time alone and sought direction, and during that time it became very clear and convincing that it was always meant to be me. It just took me a while to understand that the trip had been meant for me, and me alone, from the start.

So much in life is like that, and it's a big clue about how God speaks. You're not going to get the whole, big answer all at once, because most of us would not respond to or would shrink from that, we wouldn't be ready. The process is little by little, step by step.

Let's Talk

- ➤ What, instead of emotion, should dictate our decisions?

- ➤ What two rules did we have when riding across America that could help you to move forward in your own life?

- ➤ What question should you ask yourself when deciding how to proceed?

- ➤ What should you do when you're unsure about a decision?

- ➤ How might you take an honest assessment of yourself? (Appearance, demeanor, manner of speaking and interactions with others)?

- ➤ What ultimately determines the final outcome?

- ➤ What's really going on when people are mocking you for rising above and making personal improvements?

- ➤ What should you do if you're not clear on the reasons you're doing something?

- ➤ There are three steps to critical thinking. What are they?
- ➤ What are the dangers of allowing your critical thinking to be "outsourced"? What areas of your life might you be outsourcing currently?

- ➤ How can you improve and maximize some of the opportunities presenting themselves in your life right now?

➤ If you could "create your own culture", what would that look like?

➤ What parts of your life that you're not happy are you responsible for? What might you do to change those for the better?

➤ Why shouldn't you allow others to define who you are? If it were completely up to you, who would you be?

➤ Describe the "domino effect" of allowing yourself to become an individual.

STEP FIVE:

COMMON SENSE

When I think about common sense, I think of my sisters.

In my family, there was Mom, my older sister, Jeanette, my other sister, Linda, and me. Even though I was the "baby", I was physically ginormous, but no matter how big I was, my sisters knew I was still young emotionally and cognitively.

I can't tell you how many times my sisters threw the phrase "Use your common sense" at me. They said it all the time, and coming from Jeanette and Linda Boles, that stuck with me.

When Mom was off working one of her jobs and it was just the kids in the house, my sisters kicked up their level of thinking. They didn't leave the front door unlocked, things other kids without as much responsibility might take for granted. Over and over they'd tell me, "No, no, no, use your common sense."

That phrase provided a framework for my decision making, and thank goodness, because it's hard to find people who possess common sense these days. My sisters provided daily examples, simple solutions where the answers to problems were right in front of us and made (common) sense.

As the oldest, Jeanette was a natural leader, even when she was still just a teenager. She made sure we took the garbage out on Thursdays, that the dishes were clean, that toys weren't strewn all over the floor. She was especially thoughtful of our mom. When Mom came home from work, she had no additional worries, due to the condition of our home.

The last thing Jeanette wanted to hear from our mom was, "I've been out working two jobs, and when I come home, the place is destroyed."

Jeanette set the example, helping us to understand how to connect with and be thoughtful of people.

I got a good lesson in common sense one Sunday when I was still pretty young. I wasn't too excited about going to church that day, so I waited until the last minute to get ready. While everyone else was up, showered, applying makeup and doing hair, I waited it out.

My mom, who had the quality to her voice like Coach Mike Garland where when she spoke, that was it, said, "You're going to have to make a decision on whether or not you're going to church. If you don't go, I promise you, you're not going to like what happens."

I got up and started trying to make up for lost time, moving quickly to be ready before we had to go. Breakfast had already come and gone, so I decided to just eat a banana.

Remember those little Chiquita banana stickers? The banana had one of those on it. I peeled it off, and, still in goof off mode, stuck it onto a nearby lampshade.

At our house, things were not normally out of place. It was a home of order. Any additional, unnecessary stress being created was frowned upon. I knew that, and still I put the sticker on the lampshade. I know, idiot, right? I wasn't thinking.

My sister Linda came by, immediately noticed what I'd done, and said, "I'm going to tell you, if you don't take that off and Mom sees it, you're going to get a whoopin' right before we go to church, and you'll walk into that church crying."

I just gave her a look.

She continued, "I'm telling you to use your common sense."

As soon as those words finished leaving her mouth, my mother came out of the back room, instantly saw that sticker on that lampshade, and gave me a whoopin' right before church, and sure enough, I went to church crying.

Our world was complicated enough, without my making it more so. Common sense, had I listened to it, would have said, "Why are you putting a Chiquita banana sticker on the lampshade? That will make things look ugly, and with the heat of the bulb, that sticker could become permanent. When friends come over, they'll ask why that sticker is there, and you'll have to be the one to answer for it."

Common sense also might have forewarned me that I was already on the radar, since I'd chosen to get up at the last minute, causing everyone to have to wait for me before they could all go to church. My mother was watching me closely to see if I'd hurry to get ready and become presentable, as expected. Shoes tied, hair brushed, looking tidy. Common sense would have told me that I was being scrutinized, and that any bad decision I might make during that time would go south.

That sticker was just one more bit of evidence that I'd been goofing off, and dragging my heels.

Even as adults, we do those kinds of things. We get "stuck" in places where we're not using our common sense. And the "stickers" we get "stuck" on can sometimes look really silly.

One Saturday I was coaching my seventh grade daughter's girls' basketball team. I chose not to play one of the girls for a few very good reasons, so she was sitting it out. When her parents realized she wouldn't be playing, they were hot. On fire. Instead of having a conversation with me that went something like, "Hey, we'd really like to talk to you about this," they stood diagonally from me and tried to stare me down.

Maybe they missed the part about my being a six foot five, three hundred pound black guy that's sort of a beast. (Did they even know where I come from?)

If I'd still been "Detroit" Boles, that might have been a very, very bad situation for them. A "hey, let's take it out to the parking lot and fix this for you" sort of thing. Common sense, right?

I later talked to my staff about the situation, and the director of the club commented, "That was immature. I couldn't believe they were trying to stare you down like that."

As adults, as leaders in our communities, there are opportunities for us to be the bigger person, to process moments like that, step back to take a less emotional look at things, and just tell ourselves, "No, no, no, you don't want to act like that."

Had that couple been thinking with clarity and seeing things as they really were, they'd have noticed a large man who can carry two refrigerators, and wouldn't have been looking at me like they wanted to take it outside. Unfortunately, this wasn't a private encounter, either. All kinds of people were watching, including some very young, impressionable kids. That couple made themselves look bad, and set a poor example. And if I would have catered to that (and others had, or that couple wouldn't have tried the stare down on me), and suddenly let their daughter play, that wouldn't have been common sense on my part, either.

We really need to think about our behavior, think about how we're currently operating. Who did we learn our tactics from, and does what we're doing make sense?

Picture a family sitting around their living room together, not talking because they're all interacting on their cell phones. That's a lack of common sense, right there.

Common sense is truth that most people know under the surface, but that most people don't act upon. Again, we need to have those difficult and uncomfortable conversations, and then start doing something to change things up.

What stops people from practicing good common sense? Emotions clouding the facts that cloud the thoughts, going against the powers of reasoning, which lead to a series of poor choices.

Think about any current event; the standoffs or other violence that's coming to a head in the news, these are perfect examples of a lack of common sense. Where is the common sense in these peoples' behaviors? What could they possibly have been thinking to get into the predicaments they're now in?

The Common Sense Mantra: Emotion Doesn't Make it Right

Common sense also employs the power of reasoning. Like I said before, much of the problem involves emotions and emotion driven decisions. Just because you're emotional about something, or have a high emotional response to a situation doesn't mean that you're correct in your thinking.

A Common Sense Crisis

A worldwide common sense crisis is twofold, and not hard to picture, since we're living within it right now. For example, take a look at some of the gifts we're giving our kids.

I have a thirteen year old daughter that's been asking for a cell phone since she was eleven. She still doesn't have one, and that's in large part due to my own common sense. I look around at her friends, the boyfriends, the emotional manipulation that comes through texting from peers, and the sexting that goes on these days, plus a general lack of connectivity when a child is distracted by a cell phone. I might not be the smartest person in the world, but if my daughter had a cell phone where friends were continuously calling, she won't be talking as much to her parents. She'll also be more likely to come home from school, hop on the couch, and get on her phone with social media, texting, and other things. And if we as her parents are doing the same thing on our phones, we'll never get the chance to have a conversation.

My common sense tells me that is not what I want to create within my household, so I'll wait as long as I can before giving my daughter a cell phone, and that seems to make other people uncomfortable.

"What about safety?" they ask.

You know what? To me, safety is being able to sit down with my child at the dinner table and talk for forty five minutes, because what happens during that exchange is so powerful. I get to find out what's going on with her socially, academically, and emotionally. I get to understand and help her with any insecurities she may have. I can get a good look at her to make sure she's healthy and well. I value that time, and common sense suggests that it would be unwise to share that with an electronic device.

Why would I buy my kids cell phones, just because they and others pressured me? Because I didn't have the courage to stand up to my own children and tell them, "no"? If I want them to be happy, I'm not going to do something that I feel will create a divisive culture within our household. I need to be able to reach my kids.

Common sense also suggests that while I'm making the effort to drive my kids to school, I could also be coaching them. I'm not trying to turn my kids into all-stars, here, but the car is literally the "vehicle" to spend time with them. They don't recognize it, but, like Coach Garland, I'm being very strategic. That's when I find out how they're doing, and I might not find those things out any other way.

Why?

So I'm asking the question, "Why are people doing stupid stuff?" This stuff shouldn't even exist.

Much of it seems so simple, yet people aren't "getting" it, because as simple as it is, common sense can be one of the most difficult things to execute. For some reason it's hard for people to make that connection, and not everyone can, though the concepts are elementary.

That's what makes this conversation relevant.

When I teach workshops for adults, we have some dialogue, some laughter, and most of them leave feeling better. It's only afterward, when they go home, curl up on a blanket and have a moment of solitude where they're reflecting and gathering their thoughts that things start to get real. That's when the internal churning starts, those phrases and thoughts that begin to challenge their belief system.

How Has Common Sense Been Lost?

Where and when did we begin to lose our common sense?

That can come from running with the herd too much, something our world tries to push us to do. We're also bombarded with decision making, and there is so much accessible information out there that we rarely just take a moment to process.

When we have questions in our lives, when we need solutions, we need to be quiet and discerning. We need to pray for wisdom, and look for the simple and the obvious, instead of getting caught up in the blind spots of herd activity.

We're on social media too much, and we're allowing television to become our mentor and teacher. Is that what we want to have influencing us and the next generation? Think about it for a minute. Who are we going to choose for our mentors? Who are we going to choose to model how we want to live and what we want to become? Those people on social media or reality shows? Remember, what you take in is what you give out.

The Power of Solitude

To cultivate common sense and clear, poignant decisions, I'll say it once more, you must have solitude. Not long ago I had the opportunity to fly to India, and as good as India sounded, I had to sit with that choice for a while. Once I did, it became obvious that the same things could easily be accomplished from a series of Skype calls, saving thousands of dollars for all those involved. Had I been going by pure emotion and the excitement over visiting India, I'd have booked the flight.

Common sense isn't common sense until it's put into practice.

NOTES

Let's Talk

➤ Have you ever been in a situation that lacked common sense? Why, in your opinion, is that the case?

➤ What is the one big thing that clouds common sense? How can you stop that one big thing from clouding your own common sense?

➤ "Why are people doing stupid stuff"? What's your best guess on that?

➤ Once common sense is lost, do you believe it can be regained?

➤ What are some ways to build up your personal cache of common sense?

➤ How does solitude come into play?

CONCLUSION

How will your life story go?

If you don't like the way things are, and the life that's projected for you, like me, you have the ability to change the script. Using a little bit of courage, you can do something different. Start by loving yourself and believing (remember to talk to yourself in the mirror until you believe, and then continue to do so for maintenance), and then you'll have love to give to those around you.

When you love those around you, an entire series of new doors will open up; leading you to places you've never dreamed possible, because you're employing compassion, one of the most powerful things on the planet.

Employing compassion will build your character in ways you cannot imagine at this moment, but one day you'll get up, look at yourself in the mirror to do your "belief" statement, stare into your own eyes and know you're twice the person you once were. That will be a very good day for you.

Caring for others and having a strong character will cause you to employ critical thinking, "what might be the end result, and how might that affect me and those around me?" Critical thinking will cause you to become a wise person, and that wisdom, practiced over and over again daily, will lead to the beauty of plain and simple common sense.

With courage, compassion, character, critical thinking, and common sense, you are now ready to lead.

Start by holding up your hand, and looking at your pinky.

Enjoy the journey,
Derrick Boles

ACKNOWLEDGEMENTS

To my wife: Tanya; daughters: Jasmyne and Jayelah; sons: Javonte and Jacobie, you are my greatest blessings from God. To all my family, friends and college team mates, but especially my sisters- Jeanette and Linda Boles and my West Willow friends, thank you. To my mentors- Mike Garland, Dale Brown, Dr. Ivan Misner, Ronald Kern, Hakeem Hazim, and all of my coaches, you make me a better man.

ABOUT THE AUTHOR

Founder and CEO of the international leadership and consulting company, L.E.A.D.E.R.S.H.I.P 1st, and the nationally recognized non-profit organization, Stand Up America, Derrick Boles has been said to "embody Education, Leadership, and Inspiration." Derrick is recognized as a thought leader in human development and organizational behavior. He is also known for his expertise in leadership and for his authentic training models.

As a speaker, Derrick has reached over 80,000 people within the last year. Focused on his innovative approach to developing the "whole" individual and using what has been called his "Hearts and Minds" approach, Derrick has become one of the most sought after motivational speakers in the country. Derrick's message and his "courage to lead" have earned him national and international recognition. He has been able to build meaningful and lasting relationships with corporations, educational institutions, civil authority agencies and national youth groups which has earned him respect and the formal title as a "Leader of Leaders."

Raised in Detroit, Michigan in a single-parent household, Derrick often speaks about how his neighborhood bred violence and dysfunction, and how he was able to overcome what looked like insurmountable odds. His low socio-economic status, educational background and cultural history provided the foundation for his future understanding of a youth's need for leadership. That foundation later became the driving force behind Derrick's program, Stand Up America, whose mission is to challenge, educate, inspire and mobilize community based organizations and leaders to "Stand Up" for community empowerment. Since founding the Stand Up America program, Derrick has expanded his reach by creating adjunct programs such as, Stand Beautiful, a program for girls and young women, Men and 100 Standing, for young men. These programs are now being sought after worldwide.

Derrick's philosophy that "you can't lead unless you go first," was powerfully exemplified when he rode an ElliptiGo bicycle 1,892 miles from San Diego to New Orleans, in a call to action for communities to

A Pinky's Worth of Courage

"Stand Up" and engage in addressing those issues that plague our youth and divide our communities. Derrick's journey generated tremendous support for his Stand Up America movement and later led to a collaboration with other prominent business moguls and philanthropists.

Aside from a successful career as an entrepreneur, motivational speaker and thought leader, Derrick's passion and purpose inspired him to put pen to paper, which led to the publishing of his first book, The Courage to Lead. In keeping with his vision to educate, engage, inspire and challenge leaders, organizations and communities to infuse the character of leadership into their cultures, Derrick has launched DerrickBoles.com, which now provides access to all of Derrick's programs, products and services, and is representative of his continued expansion and growth toward global social change.

Connect www.DerrickBoles.com

Download the mobile app for inspiration and motivation:
http://derrickboles.com/mobile-app/

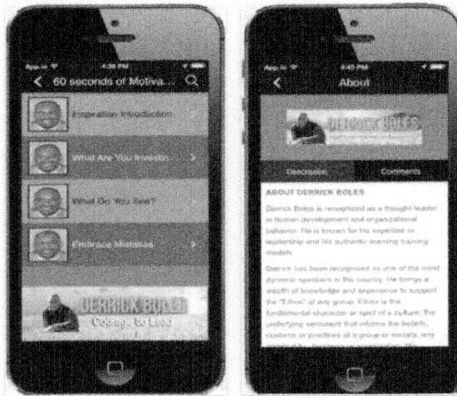

Facebook: www.facebook.com/derrick.boles.9
Instagram: DerrickBolescom
Twitter: @DerrickBolescom
Email: CEO@DerrickBoles.com

Your Reviews are highly important!
Please Review this book on
Amazon.com and GoodReads

CPSIA information can be obtained at www.ICGtesting.com
Printed in the USA
LVOW04s1548020415

433048LV00016B/1330/P